The Wally Phillips People Book

The Wally Phillips People Book

1,762,913 Heads Are Better Than One

Forwards by
Mike Douglas
& Bob Newhart

Caroline House Publishers, Inc.
Ottawa, Illinois & Thornwood, New York

Caroline House Publishers, Inc.

Library of Congress Catalogue Card Number:
79-88664

ISBN: 0-89803-012-9

Manufactured in the United States of America

For Holly, Todd, and Jennifer
What was, what is, what will be
you make worthwhile.

Special thanks to Dan Fabian—cohort, colleague, companion, and friend—whose tape recorder, typewriter, midnight oil, energy, patience, sincerity, understanding, humor, compassion, and singular writing skill made this a finished product. Without him it would have been a finished product.

Contents

Foreword

Wally Phillips and Chicago were meant for each other.

That they should come together, in the mid-50's, now seems inevitable.

Wally, with his life-long love of people. Chicago with its continuing collection of some of the most interesting and colorful people you'll find anywhere. I know. I was born there, grew up there, got my start in show business there and treasure my memories of family and friends, poor and rich, black and white, natives and immigrants—all proud Chicagoans. My kind of people. And Wally's, too.

Unlike certain celebrities who reach the heights and develop an "away with people" attitude, it's Wally's "way with people" that has brought him to the top and kept him there.

He loves people. He loves talking with them. He loves learning about them. He loves helping them.

How fortunate that he shares this love affair with so many people! In the Chicago area, daily via his two-way radio show. And, at last, everywhere through this book

about the fascinating people he has encountered in person, and on the phone: famous as well as infamous, just plain folks and notables who are bigger-than-life, individuals with clearly defined points of view and others who are puzzled and perplexed.

I fondly recall listening to Wally during my last couple of years in Chicago. These days I enjoy visiting his radio show and having him put me in touch with the people of Chicago.

Because Wally and I are both people who need people. Which as the song says, puts us among the luckiest people in the world.

MIKE DOUGLAS

"Hello, Wally? This Is Bob Newhart Calling."

. . . .

"Fine, fine, how are you?"

. . . .

"Good. Then I . . . I guess we're both fine. Well, fine. Say, I've heard that you're writing a book and that you've been trying to get up the nerve to ask me to do a Foreword for it."

. . . .

"Wally? Uh, what's so funny, Wal?"

. . . .

"I've what?"

. . . .

"I've always had what effect on you? Always been able to crack you up, I see. No, that's okay; it's what I do for a living. I was just confused because I hadn't said anything funny yet. Well, I mean I . . . never mind. Let's talk about the Foreword."

. . . .

"Wouldn't mind a bit. As a matter of fact, I think it's a darned good idea. After all, I am an ex-Chicagoan and . . . I'm sorry, I missed that. Say again."

9

. . . .

"There is no such thing as an ex-Chicagoan . . . , only what? . . . *only someone who has moved away.* A lot of that sort of thing in the book, is there? Pretty sure you wouldn't rather stick to radio? Just kidding. See, now's when you're supposed to laugh."

. . . .

"Yes, I know that you love Chicago. I do too. I was born there and I still enjoy reading about the blizzards and politicial scan . . . and everything."

. . . .

"That's true too. We really do have quite a bit in common. You're right, we're both young, handsome, intelligent and . . . sure, the telephone is a perfect example. Where would either one of us be without it?"

. . . .

"Well, no, actually I don't think that I would have been pumping gas in Portsmouth, Ohio. For one thing, I've never been there and, secondly, where would I get the gas?"

. . . .

"Yes, I knew what you meant. As I was saying, it is certainly logical for you to want some charismatic, beloved, internationally-acclaimed luminary to do something at the front of your book, and I'm the obvious choice; so let's consider it settled. Now what would you like—fifty/sixty pages, something like that?"

. . . .

"About a page and a half . . . double-spaced?"

. . . .

"Hey, it's your book! To tell you the truth, though, that will make it a little tough to get in some of the things which I had in mind."

. . . .

"Well, y'know, witty anecdotes, personal insight, little-known historical facts about the city, things like that. Baseball for instance. I've been a Cubs fan all my life and I remember one game so vividly that . . ."

. . . .

"Actually, the Cubs weren't playing anyone. It was a White Sox game, on the radio."

. . . .

"Uh-huh. Well, this was back when they used to do away games with a ticker-tape in a studio and use sound effects to make it sound as though they were really at the ballpark. This one day, for whatever reason, Bob Elson and his teletype and his crowd noises were all out of sync. See, it was funny. On one foul ball there was a cheer that would have rivaled Gabby Hartnett's home run in the dark but later, when someone tripled, all you could hear was one lonely, solitary voice shouting, 'Hot dogs. Yo! Get your hot dogs here.' Get it? Everything was backwa . . ."

. . . .

"You may be able to work it into the *blooper* chapter? Oh, right in the book. Okay. How about a Chicago story that involves my television show? You'll love this one. We had an episode in which I had treated a Cubs pitcher whose psychological problems were interfering with his performance on the mound. So then this catcher named Moose came in and . . ."

. . . .

"I really don't know what happened to the pitcher, Wally. See, I had already cured him and the rest of the show was about the catcher."

. . . .

"Well, that's just the way the show was written. No, Moose didn't have any psychological problems . . . just a

.189 batting average and a hunch that his days with the team were numbered."

. . . .

"Precisely, that's why this story is so perfect. That is exactly what I told the writers. I said, 'Look, you guys don't understand about Chicago. Cubs catchers have always hit .189, so there wouldn't be any reason for Moose to be all that uptight about his future.' They made me do it anyway. Even worse . . .''

. . . .

"I don't know why they don't actually do the shows where they're supposed to be. A lot like ticker-tape, I guess. Anyhow, in the third scene, my wife, my TV wife, and I were supposed to be watching a night game and feeling bad because the home town fans were booing Moose. Well, everyone knows the Cubs don't play at night when they're at home, so I said that wouldn't work either. The writers said they'd make it an away game. I asked why the fans would then be booing a guy from the other team who couldn't hit the ball but the writers threw up their hands and yelled, 'Do it!' We got a ton of mail from Chicago."

. . . .

"You think what?"

. . . .

"You think that's such a good story, I should save it for my own book?"

. . . .

"Sure, I've got some that aren't about baseball. I've got a couple of beautes about the hairpin turn on the elevated tracks down in the Loop. Y'know, the one that is so sharp it defies the law of gravity. Right. One time around and Sir Isaac Newton would have gone running back to his tree for more tests. For obvious reasons, every time the train would near it, I would start reading the overhead advertising cards very intently. My favorite was the one which said 'U cn Lrn Spd riting in Ls than 2 wks.' "

. . . .

"Well, no. Not you—*U*. It was. Never mind."

. . . .

"The turn stopped defying the law of gravity a while back? Yeah, that would take away some of the story's humor. Hey, how about Skid Row? Everyone can relate to that. New York has the Bowery, San Francisco the Mission District, and Chicago has West Madison. It's as American as vending machines."

. . . .

"Or . . . jogging, right. Well, I remember this one Saturday morning back when I was in high school or college. I walked by two winos in a doorway. They were fighting over a bottle, an empty bottle I think, of Virginia Dart. I overheard a snatch of conversation which will haunt me for the rest of my life because I shall never be able to figure out what could have preceded or followed it. One guy turned to the other and, through watery, bloated eyes, challenged, 'When the hell were you ever goalie for the Montreal Canadiens?' "

. . . .

"Can't use that either? Now, wait a minute, these are some classic Chicago stories I'm giving you. Like it or not, those two guys are every bit as much a part of the city as you or me or . . ."

. . . .

"The book isn't about Chicago? I don't know, I just assumed it would be. What's it about?"

. . . .

"People? Pretty broad topic, Wally. Any particular people?"

. . . .
"*All* people. Name them right in the book, do you?"

. . . .
"M-most? Tell you what. That sounds like a really terrific directory you have going there and I . . . I'd love to be a part of it but, rather than have me take up valuable space with a big deal Foreword, why don't you just ask someone to scribble in a corner of one of the pages that I, uh, I like your *People Book* a lot."

. . . .
"You bet. Anytime. Bye-bye."

Bob Newhart likes the Wally Phillips People Book a lot!

Preface

A book written by a radio guy from Chicago
is not necessarily a book about radio or Chicago.
This one, for example, is about you.

Why This Book Is All About What It's All About

Stop! Say the secret woid and win a date with the ghost of Groucho's duck. It's a four-letter job that makes everyone smile.

Not that four-letter word. This is going to be a G-rated book. Well, PG anyway, and that is the only hint I'm going to give you. Think of another one.

Was it love? Hope? Home? If so, you've already been wrong four times, and we haven't even gotten started. Try again. No, don't bother. This will be a freebie just to get us off on the right foot.

Baby.

Yep, baby. The only word in the language I can think of that always makes people feel good. The phenomenon is remarkable to watch. Carry a baby onto an elevator full of scowling, self-involved adults, and suddenly they all start making funny faces, grinning, and whispering "kootchy-koo," whatever that means. There must be something restorative about the innocence and promise of an infant's smile. Either that, or we all just wish we could go back to the time when someone else was carrying the soggy load.

In any event, during the projected 5 hours, 41 minutes, and 33½ seconds it will take you to plow through this dubious masterpiece, 2,053 American babies will be born. One thousand of them will be girls. The rest will not.

Although it may be reasonable to assume that everyone would agree to the logic of such an arrangement, two basic facts of life lean in a contrary direction. Making assumptions, reasonable or otherwise, is an invariably futile exercise, and the sum total of things upon which everyone agrees is *zero*. Take the case in point as a case in point. Surveys by the recently vocal National Gay Alliance say at least 10% of these brand new little people will grow up to be Gay. An equally vocal number of militantly straight folks say members of the NGA should quit believing their own surveys and retreat to the nearest vacant closet.

When he isn't managing baseball teams, brawling, making beer commercials or selling cowboy boots, Billy Martin agrees and disagrees strongly with both camps. Since the debate is likely to remain essentially academic for another dozen years or so, he probably has the right idea. There's a first.

Regardless of their eventual tastes in meaningful interpersonal relationships, more of these potential Einsteins, Carters, Steinems and Farrah Who-evers will be named Jennifer and Michael than anything else. We'll get into why later on. It has to do with the popularity of movie stars, records, and lots of other very scientific influences.

Like you, Jennifer and Michael will grow to be bigger, smarter and arguably better-looking than their predecessors. Jenny's bust size, for appealing example, will be about the same as her mother's, but her hips will be .6 of an inch narrower. Standing next to first Miss America Margaret Gorman, who taped-in at a less-than-contemporarily-eye-popping 30-25-32, she would look like a regular Sophia, Suzanne, Cheryl or _____ (insert the wonder woman of your choice). Infinitely more important, she will be able to stand next to and hold her own with anyone she darned well pleases. Mike won't be any slouch either. Conversant with algebra, zone defenses, and a myriad of other bits of what used to be adults-only information, he will be as tall as a medieval foot soldier and taller than Julius Caesar by the time he's eleven.

Both of them will live one heck of a lot longer as well. Whereas life expectancy for a child born in this country as recently as 1900 was only 45 years, barring excursions into excess or a leap from the Golden Gate, Jennifer and Michael will be around for 76.7 and 69.0 years, respectively. That is, of course, unless they live in Hawaii—in which case they may well last forever.

Along the way, they will:
- watch 153,000 hours of television
- have trouble spelling *pneumonoultramkroscopic-silicavoeanokoneosis, kraeusening,* and *balloon*
- consume 595 pounds of pickles, 5,390 hot dogs, 1,897 gallons of soft drinks, and 140,000 pounds of everything else
- dream of vacationing at one or both of the Disney planets
- survive 12.3 years of formal education
- love vanilla ice cream, bananas, and America's all-time favorite meal—fried chicken with mashed potatoes and corn

19

- be bombarded by 25 million advertisements
- develop 2.3 and 3.2 respective phobias and a collection of sexual hang-ups too numerous to bare
- fall in love and/or get married four times
- spend 25,000 hours in washrooms and another 203,000 hours sleeping
- have 2.2 children, a 4.4-year-old automobile, a 152-year mortgage, a googol of officially registered identification numbers, and a poodle named Fifi
- detest being called *Jenny* and prefer *Mike*, respectively
- try to make a buck
- strive for the things that money can't buy
- and die at a specific pre-determined moment.

Incidentally, exciting details of your death date are on page 135. Go ahead and take a peek, if you can stand it. On the off-chance that your bill comes due within the next week or two, you can still return this book and get a refund. Might as well. Unless you're one of those show-boats who devours a chapter a minute with your fingertips, you don't have time to finish. Besides, these days the average funeral costs a year's rent. You could use the cash.

This momentary break in the action is intended as a courtesy to those brave enough to have flipped ahead. By the time you finish twiddling and/or chewing on your hair which, in case you haven't noticed, is what you unconsciously do while reading, the survivors should be back. As long as we're killing some time, you may be interested to know that I once had an uncle who knew the exact minute of his demise without ever having to figure out any confusing mathematical formula. A judge told him.

Welcome back. That felt almost as good as walking out of the dentist's office, didn't it?

When interrupted, you were about to ask the profound question, "If life is so damned computerized and predictable, why bother to play it out?" At the risk of alienating every statistics fan from here to Valdosta, the text was about to answer with a salvo of blatantly unscientific *becauses*. Among them:

Because (regardless of how often you were told not to make waves, be seen and not heard, and all that ego-deflating trash) there is a lot more to you than a couple of bucks worth of mineral deposits.

Because you are special.

Because computers are probably too involved with what they have been programmed to consider really important stuff like processing data and having their keys punched to even bother trying to figure out what a line like "strive for the things that money can't buy" means. Of course, to be honest about it, I'm not sure we have that one down pat ourselves.

Centuries-old wisdom says there are five things in life that money can't buy:

health

happiness

a baby's smile

the love of a beautiful woman

and a ticket to heaven.

Updated attitudes narrow our non-material goals to a less pretentious field of three:

something to do

someone to love

and something to hope for.

Although both sets are desirable enough at first glance, neither could muster unanimous consent. The former probably doesn't exactly enthuse Madelyn Murray O'Hair, charter members of Zero Population Growth, or 90 percent of those people who already happen to be beautiful women. The latter list overtly discriminates against hermits, beach bums, and other self-sufficient folk. And when you get down to short strokes, neither is likely to do a whole lot for the Harold Heavybucks who inherited Uncle Louie's gold mine, or geniuses like Paul Anka who were millionaires at fifteen.

Would you settle for health and happiness?

Yes, as a matter of fact, you would.

How do I know?

I'm smart.

How did I get that way?

Simple. I listen to you.

That's why this book is all about what it's all about—*you*.

7 July 1925

Tuesday, 7 July 1925, at 2 A.M., to be precise.

Not the most significant moment in the history of the universe, but due to circumstances totally beyond my control, it mattered to me. It was the moment at which Walter Richard Aloysius Phillips began. That's right, Walter Richard Aloysius Phillips. I've never cared much for it either, but my mother had an inordinate fondness for names whose initials spelled words. Wrap was apparently the best she could come up with. It's a good thing she didn't think of Charlie.

Astrologers will tell you it was at this moment that I became a celestial Cancer, a Chinese Buffalo, and a lover of French horses. My every later move was, supposedly, predetermined by the positions of some big rocks a few thousand million miles away.

Amazing folks, astrologers. They can predict bowling averages, tell you when to stay in bed, psyche the stock market, pick your marriage partner, foresee unrest in the Mideast, and rattle off all kinds of remarkable revelations just by looking at the sky. Whenever I try to emulate their schtick,* flocks of diarrheal pigeons immediately assemble overhead for bombing practice. Of course, that's my own fault. If I had the sense to hire a certified public astrologer to give my charts the once-over, I'd know all about projected migration patterns and be able to avoid the guano look.

To be painfully candid, I don't understand astrology. I get confused by twins who live their predetermined lives in apparent contrast; by unexpected disasters which seem so predictable after the fact; by the glut of astrological/psychic/clairvoyant predictions gone awry (see page 62); by the notion that you don't get any vote in who you are or what you do.

But there certainly must be something to it. How else could so many of us from the vintage class of 1925 have contracted the same rare malady (known in advanced medical circles as congenital motormouth) over the years? Check the 1925 list of arrivals: Johnny Carson, Merv Griffin, and Mike Douglas—for openers. You must admit that is rather spooky. A host of others such as Sammy Davis Jr., Richard Burton, Paul Newman, Gwen Verdon, Angela Lansbury, Rock Hudson, Tony Curtis, Jack Lemmon, Maureen Stapleton, Rod Steiger, Dick Van Dyke, Mel Torme, Cliff Robertson, Julie Harris, and Oscar Peterson aren't all that far afield, either. Definitely a bumper crop.

Coincidence? No way! If you don't care for old movies or talk shows, blame Mars.

Speaking of birthdays, my mother was born on Flag Day, and my father was born on the Fourth of July. The script obviously called for feats of patriotic heroism on

---

* *Schtick* is show biz talk. I don't know what it means. I don't think anyone else does either, but saying it a lot makes you sound very in.

my part, so I have invested un-told hours trying to get our National Anthem changed from its present unsingable state to something that people with less than a nine-octave range can handle without risking permanent falsetto. A progress report describing my lack of progress to date begins on page 121. In the meantime, I would sincerely appreciate it if you would try to come up with the answer to one simple question. What does standing up and screeching new words to an old (olde, too, I imagine) English drinking song have to do with being proud to be an American?

It dawns upon me that, if you are an average American (average in age, that is; I know you are far above average in all other respects), you are only 29.4 years old. It must be tough for you to relate to anything as dim and dusty as the year 1925. Perhaps a few of the then-current events will provide a better handle. In 1925:

- F. Scott Fitzgerald wrote *The Great Gatsby*.
- *So Big* by Edna Ferber won a Pulitzer Prize for Drama.
- Calvin Coolidge was inaugurated for his second term as President of the United States.
- John T. Scopes was arrested in Dayton, Tennessee for violating a state law which forbade teaching the theory of evolution.
- Mrs. William B. Ross (Nellie Taylor) of Wyoming became the first woman governor in American history.
- The first dry ice was manufactured commercially.
- Flying Ebony won the fifty-first Kentucky Derby.
- A crossword puzzle fad swept the nation.
- The first National Spelling Bee was held.
- *Film Daily* critics and editors voted *Phantom of the*

Opera, Merry Widow, and *The Son of Zorro* to be among the best films of the year.

– An antitoxin for scarlet fever was prepared by George Frederick and Gladys Henry Dick of Chicago.
– Notre Dame defeated Stanford by a score of 27 to 10 in the tenth annual Rose Bowl football game.
– Bobby Jones won the U.S.G.A. amateur golf championship.
– Popular songs included: "Show Me the Way to Go Home," "Thanks for the Buggy Ride," and the ever-popular "Don't Bring Lulu."
– Army Colonel "Billy" Mitchell was court-martialed for calling military brass "incompetent, negligent . . . almost treasonable" for their lack of understanding with regard to the future of air power.
– Last, but certainly not least, Jimmy Carter was one year old. There was still time to do something about Billy.*

Expressed in computer jargon, 7 July 1925 translates to 7/7/25. Having double digits such as my pair of sevens in your birthdate is supposed to be lucky. I was, therefore, up for the big one a couple of years ago—7/7/77—my luckiest day of the century. I got some nice cards through the mail, had a piece of birthday cake with my kids, and didn't get hit by a train or suffer any other major catastrophe. Boy, I can hardly wait for the next hundred years to roll by.

No one else will be able to enjoy such an adventure until 8/8/88. Let's see, after that, 9/9/99 will be a big deal.

---

* You may be one of his detractors. You are entitled to your intelligent opinion. I shall, however, say this for Billy Carter: He never opens his mouth unless he has nothing to say.

Then the onesies and twosies and . . . gee, I feel sorry for those of you whose parents weren't farsighted enough to have planned your arrival before the thirteenth of some month.

Of course, nobody's luck can match that of Ronald R. from Newark, New Jersey. He was born at exactly 12:34 A.M., May 6, 1978 and was the ninth child in his family. All he has going for him in the numbers department is 1, 2, 3, 4, 5, 6, 7, 8, 9. If things don't work out well for this lad, we'll be able to add a zero to his string. I should probably note at this point that none of this means much of anything, but it makes for nice idle chatter at dull parties— virtually the only kind to which I find myself invited. Can I help it if I hang out with people who aren't wrapped too tight?

Speaking of nice idle chatter, lucky numbers are very big in some circles. What's yours? As yet another result of my all-important birthdate, my lucky number is four. A very significant number, four—symbolic of the four corners of the world, four strong winds, four gospels, and my golf handicap (44). Having your very own lifelong lucky number can be a big help in your quest for fame and fortune or whatever turns you on. You have one. To find it, simply add all the digits in your birthdate together. Since mine is handy, we'll use it as an example:

7 (for July, the seventh month) + 7 (the day) = 14
14 (see all of the above) + 1 (first part of 1925) = 15
15 (ditto) + 9 (second part of etc.) = 24
24 + 2 = 26
26 + 5 = 31
3 (this is the tricky part) + 1 (get it?) = 4
Shazam!*

* While I don't plan to allow any personal sentiment to enter this book, I would be remiss not to publicly credit my thirteenth grade

Enjoy numbers nonsense? If not, forget the chapter about googols. It is most definitely not for you.

Incidentally, while we're on the subject, what do the numbers at the top of the next page mean to you?

Algebra teacher, L. Hagberger, with my ability to logically lay out and explain such an intricate formula. Hope he/she is proud. (I was never really sure which percentile good old Hagberger fit into.)

1/30/33

Was it the day that:

- F.D.R. was inaugurated?
- The Senate voted to repeal Prohibition?
- The "Century of Progress" Exposition opened in Chicago?
- Katharine Hepburn, Charles Laughton, and Walt Disney won Oscars for *Morning Glory*, *Henry VIII*, and *Three Little Pigs*?
- American banks went on "holiday"?
- Primo Carnera knocked out Jack Sharkey for the World Heavyweight Championship?
- The ban on James Joyce's *Ulysses* was lifted?
- Fiorello LaGuardia's Fusion Ticket defeated Tammany Hall?
- The Chicago Bears beat the New York Giants 23 to 21 in the first National Professional Football League Championship?
- The American League won the first All-Star Baseball game?

Nope. All of those things did happen during the same year, but 30 January 1933 belongs in the books because it was the day the Lone Ranger galloped through his very first broadcast. An awful lot, including me, has happened to radio since then.

I don't honestly know if the excitement of all those thundering hoofbeats and ricocheting *ph-tings* had more of an impact on me than the millions of other eight-year-olds who were suddenly transported to those thrilling days of yore. I do know that (as he was telling his good friends Hildegarde, Cantiflas, and Efrem Zimbalist Jr. just the other day) the masked man's faithful companion is a sidekick of mine to this very moment. That's more than George Seaton or Clayton Moore can say.*

Free Bonus Trivia Insert

"Hi—yo, Silver, away!" became part of our common vernacular only because George Seaton couldn't do the originally-scripted deep chuckle in character. (Okay, now, all together—"Gosh, I didn't know that." That is why it's trivia.)

One of my least favorite activities, right up there with assembling anything so simple a child could do it, is

---

* More than I can say either, if the truth were known. I don't really have a faithful Indian companion. But I have something even better—a basketball team full of co-conspirators named John Bobera, Skip Brezinski, Bob Broz, Bob Kramer and Jim Wirth. They're my engineers, the guys who trigger Tonto's and his friends' one-liners. They're all about two bricks short of a load, but they're the best in the business.

getting out of bed at 3:30 A.M. It is also one of my more frequent activities. At the risk of sounding like a social dinosaur, I am a Morning Man. Not a Morning Person. That is someone who enjoys running around the block in a monogrammed, day-glo sweatsuit and solving three or four of the world's major crises before breakfast. I consider both of these activities demonstrably irrational behavior. You see, there are two basic kinds of people in the world. There are Larks, who like to tweet amidst the early-morning dew; and there are Owls, who like to hoot under the moon. I am an Owl, with the schedule of a Lark. Oh, well, you have problems of your own.

Morning Man is radio talk. It refers to the 6,000 or so of us who rise at ridiculous hours to help everyone else arise at a reasonable hour by going on over the nation's 6,000 or so radio stations and telling the time, the temperature, the sports scores, who hit whom with what, how bad the traffic is, and which hot new stacks of wax and tubes of tape are about to do whatever they are about to do on the charts—or, in my case, keeping Ma Bell and her stockholders happy.

At times, especially times such as 3:30 in the morning and 8:00 at night, it seems a rather strange way to make a living. But there are benefits. The pay is good—absurdly so in contrast to what schoolteachers, trash collectors, lab technicians, and other important people make. It is almost never dull and sometimes, just sometimes, it gives you the feeling that you have been in on something that matters.

Those who are paid to know this sort of thing tell me that I reach approximately 1,762,913 listeners a week. They have research books, computer print-outs, and multi-colored flow charts by the pound ("kilogram" for you trend-setters) to prove it. They are wrong. I don't reach my listeners. They reach me. More important, they reach each other. They reach each other happy and sad and angry and confused and all points in-between. As some astute, erudite, perspicacious dynamo like insurance tycoon W. Clement Stone must have once said, "That, my friends, is what it is all about!"*

It doesn't take an Ernie Einstein to figure out the equation. If the problems of being young, being old, being black, being white, being this, that, or anything else are ever going to be solved, we're going to solve them together. The second step in that direction will be understanding. The starting point is communication and that, in a small way, is where my kind of radio comes in. Trivial one minute and profound the next, People Radio is a spontaneous living mirror which can be prepared for but never really planned. It is fun, involving, informative, and without meaning to divulge Napoleonic visions of hard-core relevance to society's ills, maybe even therapeutic.

Playing word games, unraveling brain busters, collectively tsk-tsking the latest political scandal, trading ethnic one-liners, tsk-tsking same, identifying obscure movie villains, commiserating over the perpetually rotten weather, and inciting fourteen consecutive callers to discuss the relative merits of cooking Thanksgiving turkeys in or out of brown paper bags are admittedly not prime qualifications for Nobel Prize candidacy. If, however, those anonymous chefs happens to be Italian, Irish, Polish, Black, Jewish, Chicano, a new bride, grandma, a truck driver, a widower, a tax collector, the director of a grade school variety show, someone blind, or the executive vice president of some big-deal company, it seems

* W. Clement Stone ends every sentence with an exclamation point!

reasonable to suggest that there is a little more than a bird cooking. There is a genuine, bona fide, card-carrying conversation going on between some of "those" people and some of "those" people and even a few of "them." Not a meaningful debate, mind you, just a simple conversation, the everyday garden variety normal people have with friends and neighbors all the time.

The cure for cancer? No. Psychologically more nutritious than X-rated movies and chemically-induced euphoria? That sounds fair. Of course, I'm prejudiced. Unfortunately, thanks to the mental blocks and emotional filters we've been picking up since Day One, we all are.

Take this world-famous sandstone mountain for example. Do you notice anything unusual about it?

I do. I notice that it isn't a world-famous sandstone mountain. It's a picture of a meteorite crater printed upside down. Because we've been conditioned to expect light to come from above, however, it's hard to tell what this picture really is. And because of a lot of other things, we can't always see things the way they really are. It may not be our fault, but it sure is our problem.

Socially significant or not, the current state of radio stands in sharp contrast to the tired vestige of its Golden Age, into which one grizzled twenty-year-old veteran of nothing in particular and other directionless youth were falling thirty years ago. We didn't know that most smart money was getting ready to hit the lifeboats.* Oh, Fibber McGee's closet still had a few good avalanches crammed inside, and the *Amos and Andy* aberration would go right on amusing many at the expense of a few for quite a while, but radio's gilt-edged reputation as everyone's favorite free entertainment was already beginning to set as fast as the star of something called television was beginning to rise. Once the crash came, there would be some long, lean years to survive before radio finally recognized the possibility of life after ballroom remotes and emerged from its cocoon of mediocrity. Then, like now, however, it was a lot easier to see what was than what would be.

What "was" was a magical theater of the mind in which knuckles rapping a tabletop became a posse's thundering hoofbeats and bigger-than-life superstars named Major Bowes and Eddie Cantor (whom you have probably never even heard of) rolled audiences in the aisles week after week.

Families gathered after dinner to stare at the thing.

* See page 198 for gory details.

Educators bemoaned its near-hypnotic influence (are you listening Duninger?). Advertisers stood in line. It was RADIO—an American cultural institution if there ever was one. Thanks to the keen ear for talent of a dedicated broadcaster from Grand Rapids, Michigan whose far-sighted management philosophy included the hiring of almost anyone who could talk and was willing to do so sixty hours a week for $32, I was in the heart of it all. Well, not exactly the heart. With average experience of staff members in the six-month range, and a transmitter every bit as powerful as most good light bulbs, WJEF was more like the uvula.

Do uvulas still have a function? Did they ever? Let's call Ralph Nader next week and find out. We may be sitting on the makings of an expose that could blow the lid off the gargle industry and keep hundreds of dedicated young crusaders gainfully occupied for years to come.

I digress. I do that rather often. We all do. As subscribers to the *National Enquirer* and other closet intellectuals already know, losing track of original subjects is one of the many involuntary quirks we share as a direct result of the metaphysical interaction of the moon and planets—or whichever equally chic metaphysical interaction is in this month. I think bio-rhythm charting is the current biggie. Holistic food and thought are still in their embryo stages, unless you count the back-to-nature bubblegum craze we endured a while back. But I digress from my digression. In disco circles, that is known as double-dipping. In political circles, it is known as campaigning. Double-dipping has an entirely different connotation in political circles.

There I go again. Sorry. From here on out there will be, I promise you, no more tangents—an occasional tasty slice-of-life vignette, perhaps, but zero digressions. And if you believe that, I know this guy who has a mint-condition Edsel he'd love to show you.

Radio's Golden Age, the thirties and early forties, has enjoyed some fantastic PR lately. Maybe it deserved it; maybe not. If you are enthralled by nostalgia's mystique, you have probably already oohed and ahhed your way through enough glossy, hundred-pound anthologies of glorified memory to have an opinion. If not, you probably don't care. Either way is fine with me. All you need to know for the purpose of this text is that radio then was television now.

What differences existed were minor. The Mork of the day, for example, was named Buck Rogers. Jack Armstrong presaged "the Fonz" and his pals. *Saturday Night Live* aired on Tuesdays under the pseudonym of *The Fred Allen Show*. The Bickersons were prototypes of Archie and Edith Bunker. Archie, Henry Aldrich, Ricky Nelson, and Walter Denton filled *Animal House*. Everyone's favorite ex-couple, or ex-favorite couple, Sonny & Cher, were played by Edgar Bergen and Charlie McCarthy (although in Charlie's case it was easier to tell which one was the dummy). And while Ma Perkins never had anything quite like the *Three's Company* menage to contend with, her quiet little boardinghouse certainly had more than its share of clandestine goings-on going on. In fact, the only imperfect forerunner to recent video success I can think of was *Lights Out*. It was spooky and terrifying and awful, but nowhere near as spooky or terrifying or awful as *The Gong Show*, or anything else Chuck Barris has ever been a part of.

Laszlo Loewenstein (shown here on the right) and I both auditioned for a part in Casablanca. He got it because they said I looked too sinister. The fools.

Old Time Radio Freak's Quiz:

What original member of the Allen's Alley bunch is still active in the fast-paced, exciting world of broadcasting today?

Answer:
The laconic down-Easter, Titus Moody (nee Parker Fennely) is the commercial spokesman for Pepperidge Farms Baking Company. If you answered correctly, go out to dinner and buy yourself a designer scarf and musical doorbell.

My term of indenture at the voice of greater Grand Rapids only lasted a year, but I learned some important lessons for later life. I learned, for instance, how to rapidly flip more small jerry-rigged switches than I had fingers for without electrocuting myself, how not to pop *p*'s or hiss *s*'s when speaking in the vicinity of Civil War surplus microphones, and of uppermost appeal at the time, how to crack up fellow prodigy announcers while they were on the air. Off-mike idiocy, an honored tradition among even the most revered of today's somber anchor-persons, was played to world-class competition standards at WJEF. Endless fuzz-bomb sneak attacks, flaming commercial scripts, choreographed moons and the like were executed with precision far beyond our years. The knee-slapping hilarity of it all doesn't translate well to paper. Suffice it to say, my stories of favorite juvenile pranks are every bit as amusing to me and dull to everyone else as yours are.

"Yeah, but even then, how could you survive on $32 a week?" you are asking. Simple, you couldn't. There were, however, higher priorities in life than food. This was show biz! Why, I even got to do Arthur Godfrey station breaks toward the end. Besides, the station served its vast listenership and most of the alewives in Lake Michigan from high atop the one and biggest hotel in town, so the all-night binocular concession did pretty well. Not exactly Hollywood, I'll admit, but it beat heading back to Portsmouth to pump gas.

Which is not meant to imply that I never headed back to Portsmouth at all. One particular homing run stands out. Having received notice of an imminent somewhat-indelicate-to-describe but impossible-to-ignore call of nature which we all hear an average of six times a day,* I stopped at the downtown hotel and asked to use the men's room. The desk clerk shrugged and said it wasn't open yet. It was only eleven A.M. I guess I should have known better.

There are three Portsmouths in the United States, five in the world. The one in question is the garden spot of southeastern Ohio. Unless you count prime-time-only washrooms, it has precisely two claims to fame. Leonard Slye, better known in reel life to some of you older folks as Roy Rogers, was born there; and its natives don't speak with any identifiable regional accent. The local chamber of commerce made hay of the former distinction back when Roy, Dale, Trigger, and their friends were galloping through the popcorn circuit but, frankly, I don't think they've gotten anywhere near the potential mileage the latter has to offer. I mean, sounding like you're from nowhere, or not sounding like you're from somewhere, or whatever it is I am trying and failing so miserably to say, is quite a unique and prestigious thing to be able to say about wherever it is that you either sound or don't sound like you're from.

If they can ever figure out how to say it at all, Portsmouthians can say it truthfully. They are among the elite few in this entire country whose origins cannot be traced from telltale dialect. They don't "pahk the cah" like Bostonians, wobble o's like Minnesotans, have Chicago twangs, southern drawls or the Big Apple's rasp. Since local custom seldom calls for the exchange of "peace to your mantra" and "get in touch with essence" genré greetings, they can't even pass for hip, sophisti-

---

* And spend a half-hour a day responding to. At least that's the average amount of time we spend in whatever-you-like-to-call-thems.

cated California transplants. People from Portsmouth, Ohio just plain talk plain talk. It is significantly weird. It may also be one of the prime reasons why I do what I do for a living. Whereas most would-be professional talkers, especially those with network aspirations, have to work long and hard to divest their speech of geographic traits, I didn't have to do very much of anything. That worked out pretty well.

Of course, since they are all located in the same geographical region from which it would have sprung if there had been one, a hint of identifiable regional accent might have come in kind of handy while I was laboring at WSAI, WCPO and WLW. They're all in Cincinnati where I spent the next decade or so bouncing around and doing most of my serious oat sowing. Wonder how I ever missed WKRP?* From the looks of it, I would have fit right in.

---

* There really is a WKRC in Cincinnati. To my knowledge, the station's management has not yet chosen to make a lot of noise about the coincidence or claim responsibility.

8 October 1956

A talented, funny man named Bob Bell and I took Chicago by drizzle together. Our mutual boss at WLW and one of the more dynamic broadcasters you are likely to meet, Ward L. Quaal had invited us to rejoin him at the city's major independent television station, WGN (yes, the call letters *did* once stand for World's Greatest Newspaper). The game plan called for us to recreate the spontaneity and avant-garde humor of a show that had played pretty well back in Cincinnati.

𝔓𝔥𝔦𝔩𝔩𝔦𝔭𝔰'𝔰 𝔏𝔞𝔴: Things that play well in Cincinnati do not necessarily play well in Chicago. Ask any frustrated Cubs, Bears, or White Sox fan you happen to know. Scratch that. Ask any White Sox, Bears, or Cubs fan. They are frustrated by definition.

Whereas Cincinnatians had been proud and supportive of a local market production, Chicagoans wanted network slick or nothing. We apparently provided a lot of the latter. Without Bobby Kennedy and Zsa Zsa Gabor on the bill every night, our potential viewers went beddy-bye in alarming numbers. So much for Plan A.

Undaunted, Bob became the city's version of Bozo the Clown, and I became the spontaneous, avant-garde host of one of those daily teen-age dance shows that proliferated for a time while *American Bandstand* was making superstars out of anyone who visited south Philadelphia. The program's name would have made a nice trivia question to stick in at this point, but I have forgotten it. I do recall, however, that when Dick Clark learned of this competitive threat to his budding rock-'n'-roll empire, he is reported to have yawned.

Shows how much *he* knew about young people's tastes.

Robert quickly established himself as the world's leading Bozo and, almost as quickly, my teeny-bopper extravaganza was switched to nights—on radio. Imagine my excitement.

The next thing you knew, there was a nine-year wait to see the clown routine in person. Me? Two hours a night of the same tired old records, transcribed hype and blah-blah-blah I'd been tied to since puberty. It was what you might have called a low ebb.

Finally (insert a mental drum roll or trumpet fanfare for dramatic effect), someone up there decided to smile in my direction. The "up there" to which I refer was up wherever the station's transmitter was at the time. It broke. We went off the air. Talk about bottoming out—having a radio program that no one can hear is about as bottomed out as you can get. Some heavy-duty depression seemed in order, but my mood was pre-empted by a call from an angry listener on the studio phone. She complained that she couldn't hear anything on her radio. I explained the technical problem and assured her there was nothing to worry about: her set was fine; no sinister force had taken control; the world had not ended.

"Well," she demanded, "why the hell don't you make an announcement?"

My affair with the phone had begun.

And none too soon. A few more years of "happy days" gibberish and I would have been too far gone to ever turn straight. Understandably old-fashioned by today's standards, fifties-style radio was also old-fashioned at the time: dull, gratuitous, and more than a bit phony as well. The latter characteristic's most glaring manifestation was a nifty scam known as the transcribed interview.

People have always enjoyed celebrities. That is, after all, why they are called celebrities. A guest shot by Burt Reynolds, Jane Fonda, or Benji is a bankable ratings builder for any station in the country except WFMT Chicago. (Like classical music stations everywhere, WFMT is above fretting such banalities as ratings.) The problem for most radio stations during the fifties, even those licensed to serve boom markets like Cincinnati and Chicago, was how seldom celebrity-types—much less bankable superstars—dropped by for a chat. You see, way back then, celebrities lived in only two states, California and New York. Aspen, Nashville, Detroit, New Town and other current show-biz meccas were virtually devoid of celebrity status until mountain, outlaw, and soul music started making big buck waves. The vast mid-American heartland was strictly for cows and gangsters, neither of which were considered major draws on the radio.

Some overpaid public relations consultant, which means it could have been just about any public relations consultant (except, of course, a few straight arrows like Margie Korshak and Aaron Cushman), came up with the ultimate solution. Listeners couldn't see what was really happening in a radio studio, so they couldn't see what wasn't really happening there either. Voila! In place of the actual body of the hard-to-come-by bigwig, radio stations began receiving fat envelopes from movie companies, record companies, publishers, and anyone else who had a celebrity on the payroll. The envelopes contained prepared scripts full of such probing questions as, "What is the name of your new record?" The star's actual voice responded, on an electrically-transcribed disc. When announcers read the questions and played the records just right, listeners were supposed to get the impression that good old Whats-his-name and that famous celebrity were having a nice conversation right down the block at the local radio station. Once in a while the needle would skip and make it sound as though a deranged zipper had decapitated the guest, or a warped disc would inebriate the poor soul's inflections, thereby marking him or her a wino forevermore. Usually, absurdly, however, they pulled it off. There weren't many laws governing such minor technicalities as lying on the air to worry about yet, so everyone was happy. Listeners had celebrities to listen to; radio stations had the listeners (and the advertisers); and hucksters had tons of all but free publicity. Schlock!

Before going any further, I would like to explain that I started sabotaging transcribed interviews as a small but noble gesture of personal protest against the system's disregard for listeners' intelligence. I would *like* to explain it that way; but blind luck is closer to the truth. Announcing in the classic "we'll-be-back-in-a-moment-after-this-word-from-our-sponsor" style was never my long suit. I was rotten at the basics from Day One, and reached amazing depths of ineptitude whenever something mechanical went on the fritz.

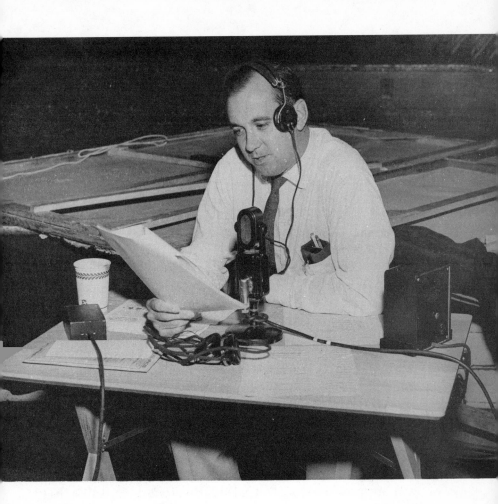

*Aspiring broadcast phenomenon, Walter Richard Aloysius—
'just call me Wrap,'—Phillips is pictured here interviewing a
well-known guest celebrity, with whom he was said at the time to
have been very close, amidst the spendor of an early big-time show
biz studio setting.*

Ah, yes, I remember it well . . . that day's penetrating question and answer cheat-sheet called for me to get things rolling by asking Woody Herman's disembodied voice how long he or it would be in town. I did. Nothing happened. Again. Still nothing. Twenty cold-sweat seconds of dead air later (the rough equivalent of the last Ice Age in the broadcast world), the needle finally tracked-down the band leader's enthusiastic reply. My next line was supposed to be, "Well, Woody, I see you've got a new hit record," to which he would respond, "In fact, ha-ha, I've got two." Stiff me, huh? "Well, Woody, you certainly do have a head on your shoulders," I blurted.

If it feels good, do it.

That felt good. Before long I was having myself one perpetual New Year's Eve of a time messing around with pretentious authors, spaced-out singers, and all manner of fellow plastic travelers.

Every time a particularly verbose incumbent senator paused for breath or dramatic effect in a campaign speech, I opened the mike and snorted.

Educators-turned-published-experts found themselves extolling the virtue of quitting school after kindergarten.

"Do you enjoy meeting all these people?" was what I was supposed to ask Doris Day. But it came out like this: "Is it true that when you and the boys in the band blow out of town on that bus, you're all boozed-up and screaming and throwing bottles out the window and beating up people in the streets? "Oh, yes, that's the real fun of it!" she effervesced.

Know what happened just when I had this revolutionary new concept in consumer advocacy programming really cooking? I got fired. That became something of a habit for a while. Fortunately, I broke it.

Interview silliness had devolved over the years into a library of brief-burst gag voices by the time my irate ladyfriend arrived on the scene. I know the transition from their artificially inseminated contributions to those of real people seems pretty obvious in retrospect, but although Steve Allen and a few others had been successfully experimenting with set-up phone calls for some time, I had frankly never given the idea much thought. She sold me. No one, not even some Edith Bunker who believes everything, would have believed her story unless they actually heard it. Next time, if there was a next time, I promised myself that they would.

My favorite true telephone story doesn't have anything to do with radio, but if I don't stick it in right here I might forget it. That would be a shame. According to a report in *Private Eye*, Mr. Frank E. Taylor, an eighty-six-year-old Hollywood resident, was arrested on charges of malicious mischief and used his one free phone call to contact Los Angeles International Airport and make a bomb threat.

On second thought, it does have something to do with radio. The phone's on-air role was, initially, that of a toy—played strictly for laughs. We had some.

"They both have terrific senses of humor, Wally. I have the number of the place where they are honeymooning. Why don't you give them a call and . . . ." A pretty rotten trick, if you ask me. The best kind.

The tenuous, groggy voice of the morning after . . . "Hello?"

"Mr. Goodman? (the name has been changed to protect the guilty) Mr. Bruce Goodman of Skokie, Illinois?"

"Yeah, who's this?"

"Freddie Finagler here, Mr. Goodman. I'm calling to . . . ."

"What time is it?"

"Quite early actually, but under the circumstances it seemed only prudent to reach you quickly. You see, I am with the Bureau of Registration. According to our records, you and a Miss Cohen received a marriage license from this office last Thursday afternoon. Is that correct information?"

"Yeah."

"Well, I am afraid there has been something of a rather unusual mistake made within our department and, uh, well the unfortunate fact is your marriage license is, uh, invalid Mr. Goodman. . . Mr. Goodman?"

"Well, it's too late to worry about that, pal."

Click.

Right about then I began to wonder if that poor girl with such a terrific sense of humor would ever again speak to her father-in-law.

Of course it was, as the man said, a bit late to be worrying about that. Especially when there were so many errands of mercy and service yet to accomplish— like calling a Chicago pharmacist on vacation out west one similarly absurd early hour to report a scandal that one of his customers had uncovered involving his store. An advertisement in his front window showed a cold capsule containing 600 tiny time pills. Microscopic inspection proved that a representative, randomly-drawn capsule held only 594. False advertising is serious business. I figured that he would want to know about the discrepancy right away so he could report it to the FDA and get off the hook.

How do you peg human nature? Here I had gone out of my way and taken up valuable time on a 50,000-watt clear channel radio station to help him avoid getting in big trouble, and he got downright surly. He recommended one of the most unique methods of introducing this cold capsule or any other medication into my system that I had ever heard. It must have been a fairly common prescription though, because the ticket manager for a major midwestern university noted for its student athletes' football prowess (I cannot legally divulge the fact that it was Bob Cahill of Notre Dame) had the same response when I reached him a week before the annual "game of the century" to order "forty seats on the forty yard line for the Forty Friendly Fellows from Freeport."

"Well, where should we go?" I entreated.

"Oh, would I love to tell you where to go," he chuckled menacingly.

Cripes, we were willing to pay!

Ben Gingiss at least had the class to pretend that his ship-to-shore radio wasn't working properly. Ben, as you may already know, is the king of the formal set. Like the soap and bra industries, the formal wear rentals business fell upon some hard times during the Woodstockian days of coverall weddings and T-shirt proms. To get his mind off things, old nose-to-the-grindstone Ben decided to take a trip. Lake Geneva must have been booked solid for the weekend, because he chose an around-the-world cruise. Well, knowing how tough it is to keep up with the local news when you're off somewhere, much less off everywhere, I thought it might be neighborly to give him a buzz. (It is probably coincidental that the phone company declared its biggest dividend in history that same day.) We tried to place the call for an entire week. He had just left his hotel in Bangkok, connections were down in Istanbul—that sort of thing the globe over. Considering the time differential, it must have been about 2 A.M. when we finally reached him on a boat somewhere between Hawaii and San Francisco. Wouldn't you know it? After all that, we'd had a slow news day. There was absolutely nothing significant to report. I had to say *something*.

"Ben, we're down at the store. Say, where do you keep the fire extinguisher?"

I was always amazed that no one ever got angry at the pranks. Certainly not my fault.

We did come close once. I placed a call to a well-known sportscaster who was covering some big-deal event in Los Angeles. Propriety and libel laws dictate that he be referred to as Mr. X. They dictate that because a female voice answered the phone.

"Hi, is this Mr. X's room?" I asked.

"Yes, it is," she cooed.

"Then you must be Mrs. X, right?"

"No," she matter-of-damning-factly replied.

Win some, lose some. I wonder if the poor guy got to watch the game before his wife's barrister showed up with the walking papers.

The experience so thoroughly spooked me that I hung up on Ed Lanctot's utterly perfect wife Pat under similar circumstances sometime later. If you know Ed (his idea of fooling around is updating the paint charts at the neighborhood True Value Hardware Store), you know I over-reacted. It is a real shame I lost my cool; I had this funny line about a fire extinguisher all set to use on him.

On it went.

There were funny calls to listeners' relatives in Louisville and Indianapolis requesting permission to camp out in their backyards during Derby/500 weeks; funny calls to gas stations asking for Ethel; funny calls to other radio stations pretending NASA was ticked because their signals were interfering with Apollo spacecraft communications. It sure beat working for a living.

Funny calls *from* people, too. Poets, inventors, philosophers, would-be activists, politicians, Cub Scout leaders with cabin fever, even the owner of a forty-year-old spaceship who kept us abreast of his comings and goings to the moon. Would the frivolity never cease?

Suddenly, or so it seemed, the day a butcher's wife called to rave about her husband's unparalleled ability to play the "meat game." The game is as old as the hills. You ask a butcher, "How's your liver today?" and he responds, "Fine, how's yours?" It sounded like an innocuous, entertaining diversion, and her husband was quick, good-natured, had an infectious chuckle, and delivered his lines impeccably. His liver was, indeed, "fine"; his kidneys "stoned"; his heart "broken." We were flapping along like a regular Martin and Lewis or Rowan or Rossi or Tut or whichever Martin and somebody-or-other comedy team you can tolerate.

"Ha, ha, giggle . . . got any brains?" I chortled.

"Brains? If I had any brains I wouldn't be in this goddamned business!"

There are some things that not even witty butchers are allowed to say on the radio. There was a big meeting that afternoon down in mahogany row. All of a sudden no one thought the panic button, for which I had long been pleading, was such a bad idea. I have never gone on the air without one again.

A lot of good it did me once word got around that fun and games with the phone could be a two-edged sword.

During one of Chicago's basic, run-of-the-mill, fifty-below wind chill adventures, I got to thinking aloud about how nice it might be to spend twenty years or so beachcombing on one of those proverbial tropical islands. To heck with snowdrifts and bread panics at the supermarket—just grab a ukelele, lie down, and suck up some serious sunshine.

"I tried," the caller said. "It doesn't work. You've got to be a rich bum or they pick you up for vagrancy and treat you like a poor one. Ever been in a tropical jail? I have—in Fiji, Pango Pango, and Tahiti. It's a bad deal all the way around."

"What are you doing now?" I asked.

"Bartending down here on the south side," he said. "Not very glamorous, but a lot safer."

The grass is always greener, I suppose.

A few minutes later another guy called and said, "My name is Art Roberts and I'm pinching myself. The most remarkable thing has just happened. I was listening to you while shaving and I nearly cut off my nose when I heard that voice. 'That's the guy!' I yelled. We've been trying to find him for eighteen years."

"You're not a Tahitian cop are you?" I asked.

"No, I'm a lawyer for an insurance company. We've been trying to find that man to settle an inheritance he is entitled to—$18,000 and the rights to a coal mine in Pennsylvania." Having assured me that he wasn't kidding, he gave me his phone number and asked me to have the bartender call him at his office later that morning. I naturally agreed and asked him to let us know how it worked out.

The next morning Art called back. "You did it. That was him," he said. Fantastic! A tingle started chilling my spine. "There's more," he said. "I don't know if he would be interested in this, but since you put it together, I thought you might like to ask him. I have a friend who owns some atolls out in the Pacific somewhere. He is always looking for trustworthy caretakers. Maybe he'd hire this guy and let him go out there and just sit on one. I'll have my friend give you a call tomorrow."

Sure enough, the next day a man called from St. Louis.

Yes, he does own a few small chunks of rock where it's always warm. There are lots of palm trees, soft breezes—the whole package. If my bartender is interested, he'll give him an interview. "Radio at its absolute best," I thought. What a simply remarkable medium! What an incredible service it had performed. I retold the entire story on the air, and rambled on for fifteen minutes or so about what a wonderful, miraculous thing this kind of radio was, and how great it was to be a part of it.

"Knock, knock."

"Who's there?"

"Pearl."

"Pearl who?"

"Pearl Harbor, sneak attack!" . . . Zonk.

The phone rang again. "Wally, I've got some more news for you about the guy who used to be a beachcomber, and the insurance lawyer, and the fellow from St. Louis."

"More?" I flabbergasted. "What more could there possibly be?"

"They're all me. I figured you've been giving it to people for so long that it was about time for you to get yours. See you on the beach."

The instinctive reaction when you've been had is to flail out at the offender with a compendium of the world's most popular obscenities, but I couldn't. The guy had done it too well. All I could manage to gulp out was, "I guess I deserved that." For once, I was absolutely correct.

In spite of nasty rumors to the contrary, that one experience was not, I repeat *not*, the reason I stopped placing put-on phone calls. Uncle Sam was. As people-radio grew more popular, its practitioners grew more numerous. A flock of disc jockeys suddenly found themselves confronted with more than twelve seconds of empty air between records. The scavenge for funny material was ruthless. Good-natured ribbing and good taste inevitably waned. Black humor and blatant intrusions on privacy became common. Frankly, the whole thing started to get a little sick.

Then, on 22 June 1970, the FCC (Federal Communications Commission for those of you who care what official-sounding initials stand for) issued a ruling called 35 FR 7732 (53:1206) 73:1206. At least, that's what I think they called it. Those FCC people certainly have a knack for naming rules, don't they? Good old 35 FR etc., read in part as follows:

> Before recording a telephone conversation for broadcast, or broadcasting such a conversation simultaneously with its occurrence, a licensee shall inform any party to the call of the licensee's intention to broadcast the conversation except where such party is aware, or may be presumed to be aware from the circumstances of the conversation, that it is being or likely will be broadcast. Such awareness is presumed only to exist when the other party to the call is associated with the station or where the other party originates the call and it is obvious that it is in connection with a program in which the station customarily broadcasts telephone conversation.

How's that for legal gobbledegook? How's that also for a way to put the crimp on funny phone calls? It's not easy to sneak up on someone if you have to tell him you are sneaking up before you begin to sneak. You vacationing pharmacists* are now on your own, so you better check those capsules out closely before you stick them in the window.

An obvious downer when it was issued, the regulation was necessary and, in the long run, quite positive. It forced us to start using the medium as a communications tool rather than a remote control whoopee cushion: to stop treating each other as jokes and begin again as human beings. Not a bad change of pace.

* Speaking of pharmacists, did you know that in Utah it is illegal to sell gunpowder as a headache remedy?

The Language
Lesson #1

Never End a Sentence with a
Preposition

Football players' occupational hazards weigh 267
pounds and sport lethal headgear. Police and other
shift-workers are regularly irregular. Letter-carriers face
rain, sleet, snow, dark of night and Fido. The banes of
radio announcers' existences are the militantly literate
who notice and call outraged attention to sentences that
end with words like with.

"Do not," I have more than once been told in terms
most certain, "end a sentence with a preposition."

Which brings to mind the story of the small boy who
did so incessantly, much to the chagrin of his father the
Language Arts Instructor (English Teacher to you old-
timers). After one particularly grievous transgression at
the dinner table, the boy was sent to his room empty-
bellied to repent. The youth's mother, while she agreed in
principle with the need for proper communication skills,
suggested that her husband had, perhaps, been too
harsh. He concurred and, as a conciliatory gesture, went

to the boy's room to kiss him good-night and read him a bedtime story. Seeing the ominous figure at his door and fearing the worst, the boy blurted, "Whadja bring that thing to read to me out of up for?"

The father was last seen racing barefoot down the median strip of a major interstate highway screaming Burma Shave limericks at the top of his lungs.

Moral: Never end a sentence with a preposition if your father really doesn't want you to.

The Mystery
Of The
Little Black Box

Approximately three minutes after the occurrence of any disaster, someone calls to report a neighbor's sister-in-law's hairdresser's hot rumor that some world-famous psychic warned his or her boss of the big explosion at the marshmallow factory or whatever it was twenty minutes before it happened.

Frankly, that makes me uncomfortable. Don't get hostile. I said uncomfortable, not nauseous. I do not want to call anyone's neighbor's sister-in-law's hairdresser, or any world-famous psychics, or their secretaries, or tea-leaf readers, phrenologists, bio-rhythm experts, astrologers, clairvoyants, or any other seers of the future (especially my friend The Wizard of Odds, Jimmy the Greek) fibbers. Yes, I agree that continued scientific investigation of the human brain's potential is a fine idea.

If, however, an elite few mental giants already possess some extraordinary powers, why aren't they using them to help us cerebral midgets sluff through? Why aren't they warning us to keep an eye on the Jim Joneses, DC-10's, and our leaky nuclear reactors, or helping Dr. Salk find the cure for cancer? Why are they so fixated upon jet set couplings, Jackie's every move, and the ability to play parlor tricks with car keys?

Take Irene Hughes, for example. Please.* Irene, as you may recall, is the world famous psychic who predicted a big Chicago snowstorm in January of 1967. There was, as you may also recall, a big Chicago snowstorm (the biggest, in fact—24 immobilizing inches in one massive splurt) in January of 1967. It might have been more impressive if she had worked it all out for June of 1967, or also warned us of the '79 machine-wrecker, but that one it's-going-to-snow-this-Friday gig was enough to earn Irene her permanent place of honor in the hierarchy of local seerdom. Along with other world famous psychics such as Jeane Dixon who predicted Ethel Kennedy's remarriage, Kebrina Kinkaid who predicted Ethel Kennedy's remarriage, and Eva Petulengro who predicted Ethel Kennedy's remarriage, Irene has been exercising her special powers to predict things for fun and profit ever since. Just to give you an idea of how fantastic they have been, here is a random sampling of some notable predictions:

JEANE DIXON, the world's most phenomenal seer, a self-professed messenger of God, and a modern day Nostradamus whose (to quote the *National Enquirer*) "uncannily accurate prophecies have stunned America." Her predictions follow:

1969 - Ethel Kennedy will remarry.

1970 - George P. Shultz will emerge as a great national leader.

---

* 'What," people seldom ask, "is Henny Youngman really like?" "Unilateral," I reply.

Ralph Nader will be the victim of a meat/food expose.
Ethel Kennedy will remarry.

1972 - Frank Sinatra will go into religious work.
Coach George Allen's future is red roses.
Ethel Kennedy will remarry.
Hugh Hefner "has a fabulously favorable aura around him. In 1973 he will go into local politics in Chicago. His wealth will grow remarkably; his real estate holdings will bring fantastic returns."
(Author's note: This passage proves beyond doubt Mr. Hefner's oft-rumored nasty streak. He obviously moved to California, caused *Playboy* stock to temporarily plummet, and had it blamed on the corporation's questionable real estate investments just to embarrass Mrs. Dixon.)

1973 - Fidel Castro will fade from political sight.
Minor troubles will arise here and there, but nothing major involving the United States will happen until 1975.
Ethel Kennedy will remarry.

1974 - A resignation or impeachment is not in Richard Nixon's stars. (Must have been a foggy night.)

1976 - Nelson Rockefeller will become "caretaker President" after Gerald Ford resigns.
No later than August 1977, super advanced humans from a hidden planet on the other side of the sun will land on Earth and begin giving us telepathic help in overcoming all disease, starvation, and war.
(Author's note: This shattering vision came as a result of

Mrs. Dixon having made a wish upon a star while standing in her garden one night. It apparently so befuddled her that she has forgotten to predict Ethel Kennedy's remarriage ever since.)

1977 - Terrorists will seize and blow up a New York skyscraper.
A new superstar will emerge from *The Gong Show*.
America's space shuttle will crash.
Russia will perpetrate history's first space hijacking.

1978 - A new pope will take office within the next four years, but not in 1978. Pope Paul will surprise the world with his vigor and his determination.

1979 - Rosalyn Carter will have an active diplomatic year, making several trips for her husband.
Comedian Robin (Mork) Williams will enjoy success.
Gerry Ford will be in demand as a Republican strategist.
If she keeps in good spirits, Patty Hearst will have her heart's desire by November 1982.
(Way to go out on a limb, Jeane.)

The top banana in any field is subject to intensive scrutiny and controversy. Such has certainly been Mrs. Dixon's lot. Some of her statements ("I'm not looking for fame; I'm not looking for any glory . . . all I want to do is help mankind help themselves"), especially those indicating that she has never used her God-given gift for personal profit and gives everything she earns as a public person to charity, have courted debate. I do not intend to become involved. I honestly don't have any idea whether or not she is really fourteen years older than she claims, was once married to someone named Charles Zuercher, or ever planned to become a nun. Frankly, I do not care.

I do care about allegations made in the *Washingtonian* a few years ago that her much-publicized Children To Children Foundation was a tax shelter for her business activities. Even if this is true, the magazine's indictment that less than 20% of the foundation's annual revenue is ever distributed to "Miscellaneous Child Care and Education" is potentially misleading. After all, it is not easy or inexpensive to operate a legitimate charitable organization. Look at the administrative overhead built into The Neediest Families Fund right here in Chicago. No, on second thought, better not—there isn't any. The UNICEF Fund? No. CARE? No, I guess that one's pretty clean, too. Hmmm.

JEROME GRISWELL is a world famous astrologer (incidentally, never call an astronomer an astrologer unless your Blue Cross premiums are paid) whose prophecies include:
  – Leaning Tower of Pisa will collapse.
  – King Charles III will have a sex change operation.
  – In 1973, a stinging rain will fall, killing everyone on a small island near Greece. It will remain a mystery until it is found to be a new weapon operated by enemies from outer space.
  – Ireland will lay claim to Britain on 17 March 1980. (Now, that's what I call a St. Patrick's Day Bash!)

CARROLL RIGHTER is syndicated in over 350 newspapers. He has predicted dozens of neat things, including Farrah Fawcett-Majors' baby in 1976 and irrefutable proof of alien life-forms by 1980.

FLORENCE VATY, the world famous Los Angeles

psychic, is said to have predicted Nixon's resignation (Wow!), Charles Manson's 1978 escape from prison, and the death of Alexander Onassis. (She may also have had something to say about Aristotle Onassis, but I could not find records.)

URI GELLER, the Israeli super-seer, is best known for his ability to bend silverware by remote control. Like Mrs. Dixon, he has had close encounters with visitors from space. He also admits that his power comes from outside intelligence, and has received specific input from the spaceship *Spectra* and an unearthly computer called *Rhombus 4-D*. He predicted the imminent arrival of UFOs in April 1975. He is also known for his tempermental walk-outs on anyone questioning his power. (Could it be Rhombus at work?)

MAURICE WOODRUFF's credentials are unknown, but if he's big enough to have predicted Ethel Kennedy's remarriage, he's big enough for me.

ARLENE ADAMS, a clairvoyant grandma from California, predicted in 1975 that Nancy Kissinger would leave Henry after scandal forced him out of office.

SHAWN ROBBINS, world famous New York clairvoyant, has this to say:

1974 - Watergate will not affect Nixon.
       Queen Elizabeth will abdicate by 1976.

1976 - A Big Foot monster will be captured in November 1977. Using sign language, it will explain that it was left behind by aliens from another planet. (Shawn must get vibes from Six Million Dollar Man reruns.)

1979 - Rock Hudson will disappear, then show up three weeks later working as a farmhand with amnesia.

OLOF JONSSON, in 1979, made this prophecy: Debbie Reynolds, mother of Carrie *Star Wars* Fisher, will launch a TV comeback with a science fiction show that will be even more popular than *Battlestar Galactica*. (Of course, watching parakeets eat is more popular than that extra-terrestrial turkey.)

EVA PETULENGRO, the world famous British as-trologer and seer, forecasted the Beatles' 1972 reunion and the aforementioned good news for Ethel.
(Author's comment: I sure wish Ethel would cooperate. Look at all the nice people she is keeping from getting world-famouser by playing so hard-to-get.)

DR. JOSEPH JEFFERS, the world's foremost LBJ look-alike psychic, who has earned doctorates in religion, philosophy, and the ever-popular eschatology and been a guest on more than 30,000 radio and TV programs, excluding mine, intoned the following: "There will be only one television network by the end of 1976." (Prom-ises, Promises.)

KEBRINA KINKAID, Hollywood's "Psychic to the Stars":

1976 - Forced school busing will be abolished.

1977 - The Air Force will reveal capture of a UFO and its humanoid passengers.
Patty Hearst will be engaged to the son of an influ-ential American publisher.

1979 - Tony Orlando will make a big TV comeback in a religious show.

FREDERIC DAVIES, New York's foremost astrologer/ psychic:

1976 - Johnny Carson retires to become a full-time minister.
Lucille Ball becomes ambassador to an undisclosed Asian nation.

1977 - Henry Winkler will quit *Happy Days*.
Freddie Prinze will be the father of twins.
An unmanned spaceship from another planet will crash in Arizona.

1979 - Lorne Greene will be visited by beings from another planet.

DAVID HOY, world famous etc.:

1976 - Big news will be made in women's pro tackle football. A league will be formed.

MRS. BRYANT (no bio available) predicted that scientists will discover an herb growing in the desert that has remarkable curative powers.

MARJORIE STAVIES, a biggie, foresaw, in 1976, massive earthquakes in California that would rip apart mountain ranges and reveal the biggest gold deposit ever. (She did not indicate if the strike would be called the San Andreas Vault.)

With apologies to crime fighter Peter Hurkos, Akashan, Ed Snedeker, Miami's Micky Dahne, Daniel Logan, Gary Wayne, Buford Georgia's Ellen Evans, Dr. Joe Pinkston, Jos DeLouise and all the other world famous prophets who probably already know I don't have the time or inclination to highlight their incredibly accurate predictions, I've saved the best for last. Ladies and gentlemen, without further ado, I present the record of Chicago's very own psychic favorite daughter IRENE HUGHES:

1968 - George Romney will be elected President.
    Mayor Daley will not be re-elected in 1971.
    The Cubs will make it to the World Series. (Hope they had good seats.)

1971 - Mao Tse-tung will die by August 1972.
    Nixon will not be re-elected in 1972.
    Red China will attack the U.S. by 1973 or 1974.
    Vietnam will be over by 1972.
    World War III will begin by 1974 at the latest.

1975 - Respected scientists will conclude that sightings of a ghost in the White House are genuinely paranormal. (Certainly sounds paranormal to me.)
    Inflation will ease; food and fuel prices will begin to fall.

1976 - Johnny Carson will leave *The Tonight Show* following a bitter dispute with NBC.
    Prince Charles of England will be lost at sea, but found still alive.
    Fidel Castro will be ousted as Cuba's premier.
    Gerald Ford's son, Steve, will become engaged to a famous country and western singer. His sister Susan will wed, but not in the White House. (She must not care for ghosts.)

1978 - A former congressman's mistress will say some things about Richard Nixon that may not be true.

Halfway through 1979, it seems that Irene has decided to play out her option. All of the pulp sheets have suddenly stopped blasting "IRENE PREDICTS" in their headlines. No news is good news, I guess.

Wally's Believe It if You Want to!

According to Professor Benjamin Burak of Roosevelt University, on the afternoon of Chicago's 1967 superstorm, world famous psychic Irene Hughes, credited with having predicted same, drove a distance of approximately twenty-five miles from her Chicago Heights home to the University of Illinois Circle Campus, where her car became stranded in a snowdrift.

THE MYSTERY OF THE LITTLE BLACK BOX

I evidently missed the follow-up articles which revealed why none of these predictions seemed to occur on schedule and why a few little things like Iran and Uganda weren't mentioned. My track record in that regard is abysmal. I do much better with the prognosticatorial vibes (I call your attention to my adept use of the inside jargon. Seers are said to be very fond of buzz words such as "impressions" and "vibes.") that come to spectacular, normally cataclysmic fruition. Someone's hairdresser's sister-in-law's neighbor usually lets us know about them right away.

Enter the little black box.

Over the years, people began to think that I was doing the supernatural folks a disservice by never giving billing to any of their *correct* predictions before the fact. "Why," they asked, "don't you ever mention some of those fantastic correct predictions before they come true so we can all be impressed when they do?" Frankly, I could never figure out how to accommodate this request. Until, that is, it finally came to me, as if in a vision from outer space: "Why not set up a controlled scientific experiment—one designed to give those of us who haven't been endowed with any special powers a glimpse of the miraculous process at work?" "Sure we can use Uncle Harry's barn as a theater, and get the old gang back together again to paint the stage, and . . . ." (Are you thinking of one of those great old let's-put-on-a-show movies starring Mickey Rooney that Channel 9 reruns twice a week? The mind is a delicate instrument. Better empty yours before we go on. Try concentrating on all of the smart things you've ever heard David Susskind say. That should do the trick.)

Where were we? Oh, controlled scientific experiments. They are ennobling adventures; they make you feel like Pasteur or Edison or Henrietta Brokenbow. Remember Henrietta? She suggested one of my all-time favorite controlled scientific experiments—the one with the plastic pyramid and the apple. We darned near rediscovered penicillin that time. Probably would have too, if the radio station's narrow-minded building manager hadn't done his Mr. Whitman imitation and threatened to call in the sanitation department.

The subject of the experiment in question is telepathic communication. While modern prophets come from a wide variety of specialty fields, they all seem to have a knack for this nonverbal conversation. So I put a piece of paper inside a little black box. The piece of paper has a name written on it. No one tricky, just a living person who popped to mind. It appeared, at the time anyway, that this experiment would provide a unique opportunity for one and all to show their stuff.

As per detailed instructions from some scientific-types who know all about this sort of thing: every once in a while I dim the studio lights, ask my record turner since childhood, Fred Keller, to play some innocuous music, and concentrate as hard as I can on that name. I close my eyes and repeat it over and over and over. What is supposed to happen next seems fairly simple to me, but what do I know about the unknown? Irene or one of her

Here you see fellow investigator Jackie Coogan and I running a controlled scientific experiment designed to discover whether things fall on people who walk under ladders. No such luck. Coogan is pictured under the ladder. I do not recall the other investigator's name.

equally-gifted cohorts should tune in on my transmission, call, and with appropriate solemnity, announce, "The name in the box is. . . ."

All the rest of us immediately gasp.

Heraldic horns blare all over town.

Steeple bells clang.

Tons of confetti fall onto the streets that Heronner's emergency crews have just cleared of last January's annual unexpected precipitation.

A caller suggests that the confetti be used to fill potholes and immediately cracks up in admiration of his own originality.

We realize, once and for all, that those who doubt are charlatans of the lowest order. This is especially true of the misguided magicians who dare to re-create Uri Geller's inexplicable bending key phenomenon as a cheap theatrical trick. What a rare and thrilling opportunity to expand the horizons of all personkind, to help bring justice, truth, and the alien way to the fore.

So why has it been such a dud? Why have I spent the last several years mumbling in the dark like a big dummy without so much as a hint of success telephathy-wise? Why have all the big time psychics assiduously avoided me while their amateur counterparts give the guild a bad name by guessing wrong time after time?

Is the dollar-a-day prize that will go to whoever identifies the mystery name too puny to warrant serious consideration? Are quarks from space messing up my transmissions? Is my microphone blocking your view? Do I have a defective little black box? Or, shudder and furtive glance, is it me?

In desperate hope of ending the embarrassment of my inadequacy as a medium, not to mention the tedium, I have devised a new four phase plan to remedy the situation:

Phase 1: More Convenient tune-in times.

From now on, I'll begin my heavy-duty concentrating at precisely 10:32:14 A.M. on the first Tuesday of every month.

Phase 2: Ease of Response.

Simply snip out and send in the handy entry blank which follows.

Wally Phillips

WGN-RADIO

2501 West Bradley Place

Chicago, Illinois 60618

The name in the Black Box is:

_____

My name is

_____

_____

_____

_____

Date _____

Phase 3: A Fatter Pot.

The first psychic, pro or amateur, who gets me, figuratively, and the mystery person, literally, out of the box will now win $5,000. (Barring a continuation of runaway inflation, this ought to be enough for dinner for two at the restaurant of your choice—except, of course, The Palace in New York.)

Phase 4: Cheating.

The name is not only in the box; it is also somewhere in this book. Some wheres, actually. I don't want to insult your powers by making this too easy, so I've put the first name in one place and the last name in another. Be the first to find them and get the goodies. In the event of a tie, we'll split the pot. Act today! When the name is revealed, anyone who says, "I knew it all the time" will be chortled at heartily. Universal fame and adulation await the winner. Five big ones too. Someone may even say your name on *Saturday Night Live* or the *Mike Douglas Show*. *National Lampoon* could buy the rights to your life story for its next implausible smash after "Jaws Meets Animal House". This is major material. Act *now!*

Cleverly Concealed Secret Message
C'mon, Jeane. Give me a break. Tell you what. Get me off the hook on this thing with the name in the box and I'll propose to Ethel Kennedy for you.

Second cleverly concealed secret message:
How about you guys from outer space? Want to pick up a few quick earth bucks for some souvenirs or something? For you, they'll even be tax free unless you use them to find oil on some asteroid. Look, if you're so big on telepathy, why don't you prove it? Pretty please? Nanu, nanu, and shazbut? Win one for Mr. Spock?

With The Rodrigo Could Have

"Blindfolds in place? All right, will our mystery guest kindly enter and sign in please."

So began the weekly high spot of one of the longest-running programs in the history of television, *What's My Line?* Contrary to general misconception, *Meet the Press* is TV's all-time longevity champ. *Gomer Pyle* only seemed interminable.

In order to maintain suspense and protect the show's integrity (game show producers were very big on integrity) during the early days of television), visiting celebrities' trick voices occasionally stumped the panel. They should be so lucky with you. No one's true identity has ever eluded your penetrating ear. Let's see how well you do with no voice at all.

Right Agent,
De Triana
Been A Star

I have in mind the name of an extremely popular entertainer whose initials are F.S.

Known primarily as a singer, FS's multi-faceted career began during the Big Band Era.

Our mystery guest was once amorously linked to a famous dark-haired Hollywood sex symbol.

The first name is of Teutonic extraction and originally meant "free."

FS's recent success has tasted particularly sweet because it came in the wake of premature retirement from the public eye.

Who is FS?

The correct answer is FANNIE SHORE, of course.

You would be amazed by how many less perceptive people thought it was Frank Sinatra. Not only that, would you believe that they are all pouting and screaming "foul" right now, just because they happen to know Fannie as Dinah? Tough! This is the major league, and the sooner they learn it the better. Everyone should know that any mystery guest worth the billing has had as many name changes as nose jobs. Well, not that many, but at least one. I won't bore you with the entire scroll, but as a conciliatory gesture to the uninformed, a few notables follow:

Woody Allen	Allen Stewart Konigsberg
Harold Arlen	Hyman Arluck
Charles Aznavour	Varenagh Aznaourian
Anne Bancroft	Annemarie Italiano
Orson Bean	Dallas Frederick Burrows
Warren Beatty	Warren Beaty (that hardly seems worth the trouble)
Joey Bishop	Joseph Abraham Gottlieb
Yul Brynner	Taidje Kahn, Jr.
Ellen Burstyn	Edna Rae Gillooly
Wendy Carlos	Walter Carlos
Vicky Carr	Florencia Bisenta de Casillas Martinez Cardona
Cyd Charisse	Tula Ellice Finklea
Joseph Conrad	Teodor Jozef Konrad Korzeniowski
Alice Cooper	Vincent Damon Furnier
Rodney Dangerfield	John Cohen
Doris Day	Doris von Kappelhoff
Sandra Dee	Alexandra Zuck

Kirk Douglas	Issur Danielovitch
Diana Dors	Diana Fluck
John Denver	Henry John Deutschendorf, Jr.
Mike Douglas	Michael Delaney Dowd
Bob Dylan	Robert Allen Zimmerman
Tom Ewell	Yewell Tompkins
Mama Cass Elliot	Ellen Naomi Cohen
W. C. Fields	William Claude Dunkenfield
Dame Margot Fonteyn	Margaret Hookham
Judy Garland	Frances Gumm
Samuel Goldwyn	Samuel Gelbfisch . . . (Metro, Gelbfisch, Mayer?)
Cary Grant	Archibald Leach
Lee Grant	Lyova Haskel Rosenthal
Jean Harlow	Harlean Carpentier
Laurence Harvey	Larushka Skikne
William Holden	William Franklin Beedle, Jr.
Kareem Abdul-Jabbar	Ferdinand Lewis Alcindor, Jr.
Boris Karloff	William Henry Pratt
Ann Landers	Esther "Eppie" Pauline Friedman Lederer
Frankie Laine	Frank Paul Lo Vecchio
Lao-tzu	Li Erh . . . (maybe it was the other way around)
Jerry Lewis	Joseph Levitch
Peter Lorre	Laszlo Loewenstein
Bela Lugosi	Arisztid Olt
Ray Milland	Reginald Truscott-Jones
Marilyn Monroe	Norma Jean Mortenson

Yves Montand	Ivo Livi
Bill Moyers	Billy Don Moyers (if he had left it alone, he'd probably still be in Washington)
Mike Nichols	Michael Igor Peschowsky
Merle Oberon	Estelle Merle O'Brien "Queenie" Thompson
Stefanie Powers	Stefania Zofia Fererkiewicz
Debbie Reynolds	Mary Frances Reynolds
Mickey Rooney	Joe Yule, Jr.
George Sand	Amandine Aurore Lucie Dupin, Baronne Dudevant
Beverly Sills	Belle "Bubbles" Silverman
Phoebe Snow	Phoebe Loeb
Joseph Stalin	who cares
Connie Stevens	Concetta Ann Ingolia
Sly Stone	Sylvester
Tiny Tim	Herbert Buckingham Khaury
Abigail van Buren	Pauline Esther "Popo" Friedman Phillips
Jersey Joe Walcott	Arnold Raymond Cream
Clifton Webb	Webb Parmelee Hollenbeck
Flip Wilson	Clerow Wilson
Shelley Winters	Shirley Shrift
Stevie Wonder	Steveland Morris Hardaway
Natalie Wood	Natasha Gurdin

And who could ever forget the lovely and talented Spiro Anagnostopolous?

Smart-off columnists with short hair and names like Mike and Royko say that the celebrities' penchant for

Illinois Governor, James "Big Jim" Thompson explains the intricacies of his presidential non-candidacy to everyone's favorite centerfold (pictured in mufti arear) as Milton Berlinger dozes enthusiastically.

name conversion is nothing more than an expression of their vanity. Nonsense! An on-target alias is every bit as important to a person's career as a good agent, a Japanese gardener, and an annual sabbatical at the fat farm; it is essential to the development of a correct public image.

After all, this is the real imaginary world we're talking about—a publicist-eat-publicist jungle where some names just don't make it. Think about it. How could all of those socially significant gossip magazines have survived the ravages of time and *Time* if they had had nothing but the latest hot scoops about Edwin Fisher, Mary Frances Reynolds, and Concetta Ann Ingolia to report? Could Leslie Townes Hope have been as funny as Bob? Would Frank Cooper have stood as tall in the saddle as Gary? Would Vincent Damon Furnier be anywhere near as gross as Alice Cooper?

Would Shock Theater's late night horror flicks have been as scary if they'd featured Willie Pratt, Laszlo Loewenstein, and Arisztid Olt instead of Boris Karloff, Peter Lorre, and Bela Lugosi? Pratt, Loewenstein and Olt? Passers-by would have thought the Bijou had become a kosher deli or a hangout for wayward Certified Public Accountants.

Face it. Names matter.

Quick, would you rather have a blind date with someone named Waldo or Richard? Gertrude or Melissa? Who is the better athlete—Percy or Kevin? The better dancer—Bertha or Michelle? Is Irving or Joe more likely to be a professor of economics? Who has the most friends—Adolph, Agatha, or Kim? Do you have any mental picture of people named Basil, Thelma, or Beauregard? Of course you do.

The value of a well-chosen pseudonym is by no means a

concept exclusive to image-conscious stars.* Embezzlers, writers, politicians, and other unsavory characters have been dabbling in identity re-cycling for years. In fact, mothers of movers and shakers in every conceivable field of endeavor once knew their children by other names. Geronimo was actually Goyathlay to his merry band of renegades. Vladimir Ilyich Ulyanov (you know him as Lenin) spearheaded the Russian Revolution. Even old Sigismund "Get-your-head-screwed-on-straight" Freud was a little neurotic about his label. No sooner had he shrunk it to the more macho-sounding Sigmund than, *pow*, he was the father of a whole new branch of medicine.

Mr. Freud, incidentally, was bullish on dreams. Not at all like our current mind-bender, Werner Erhard, in that regard. Werner, as you had better know by now, is the forceful chief guru and founder of EST. His second debut (third, if you count a brief adventure as Jack Frost the used-car salesman) was calculated from the word go. Thanks at least in part to the efforts of his ace advance man John Denver, Werner has been able to rent hotel basements all over the country to sell his notions of serenic destiny control via stoic toilet training with phenomenal success.

He readily admits (being able to readily admit things is evidently one of the foremost benefits of EST training) that his success would not, could not, have happened with timid construction superintendent Jack Rosenberg at the helm. "I just wanted to get as far away from Jack Rosenberg as I possibly could," said Werner at a rare lucid moment. I, for one, can certainly relate.

---

* Even towns have gotten into the act. Eleva, Wisconsin, for example, was re-named by a sudden snowstorm which permanently interrupted the painting of a sign that should have read "elevation" on the side of its large water tower.

Little Known Fact

If Julie London had married Lloyd Bridges instead of the horn player, divorced him and married famous attorney William Fallen, then divorced him and married Hugh Downs, her full name would have been Julie London-Bridges-Fallen-Downs.

Believe it or not, I am trying to make a point. Names have a direct effect upon the way people see you and the way you see them. They should, *must*, be chosen with care.

Adults have had time to give the matter some thought, and they can appeal to the courts or studio management for a new identity. But what about babies? They get no say in the decision, and they have to live with it. As often as not, they wind up with a name that doesn't fit their personality, or is simply all wrong for their ultimate goals. Some misnomers even seem blatantly intentional. Why else would real people be called Magdakeba Babblejack, Lester Chester Hester, Effie Bong, Twila Delilah Blonigan, Armand Hammer, Scoot A. Long, Esophagus Brown, Dillon C. Quattlebaum, Mary Hatt Box, Bertha Big Foot, Singular Onions Gallyhawks, Juliet Seashell Moonbeam Gamba, John Will Fail, Strange Odor Andrews, Heidi Yum-Yum Gluck, Wava White Flagg, Ima June Bugg, Mary Rhoda Duck, or Penelope Palm Tree Groves? Those are real. Most are innocent enough. Some, especially John Will Fail, are plain sick. Anyone who would hang that kind of albatross on a child deserves to be tied to the rear fender of a '57 Chrysler and forced to listen to three weeks of uninterrupted Blues Brothers music.

Please, the next time a stork or faulty prescription drops a decision in your lap, give the kid a break. Don't leave the name choice for a frenetic delivery room coin toss. Give it some thought. You will, in a very real sense, be determining who and what your child will become by the name you give it. That is, of course, if the heavens allow you to make the choice. You see, it really depends on where Pluto and Saturn are, or were, or might have been when the baby, or you, or someone else was either conceived or born—unless the wind was blowing south and your rhythms were in sync—unless, perhaps, this naming influence has veto power over other governing influences because it comes later in the book. Got that? Call Irene or Jeane for the details.

In the meantime, I'll work on the assumption that we do get first pick.

If you want to stack the odds in favor of your kid being a lawyer, a doctor, or a basketball player, pick a lawyer, doctor, or basketball player's name. It worked for Dustin Hoffman's parents. They named him after the silent movie cowboy star Dustin Farnum. Fortunate for Dustin that they weren't as overly fond of stuntman Yakima Canutt. Fortunate all the way around, in fact. A wrong given name just has to be changed when its bearer grows up and picks a role. That it is expensive, wastes valuable time in our efficiently run courts and gives people fits when they try to identify mystery guests in later years.

Selecting the right name needn't be too difficult a project. Library shelves are full of books on the subject. They cover the dynamics of naming, the history of names, probable future character traits, etymology, onomatology, and lots of other nice "ologies" which are no doubt meaningful to someone.

One particularly good reference piece on the subject was written by an associate editor of *People* magazine, Christopher P. Andersen. Named *The Name Game*, it plays games with names. One game asks you to match thirty-two common first names with adjectives.

According to Mr. Andersen, a psychologist named Ralph Winsome, who probably also loses some, asked 1,100 people to play the game in 1973 and came up with the following matches. What do you think?

Allan	Serious, sincere, sensitive
Andrew	Sincere but immature
Anthony	Tall, wiry, elegant
Benjamin	Dishonest
Daniel	Manly
Dennis	Clumsy
Donald	Smooth and charming
Edward	Thoughtful
George	Aggressive
Gordon	Hardworking but unsuccessful
Harold	Coarse
Hugh	Mediocre
Joseph	Intelligent, earnest but dull
Keith	Hard, self-reliant, ambitious
Mark	Spoiled
Paul	Cheery, honest and proud
Richard	Very good-looking
Robert	Diffident
Roger	Red and plodding
Simon	Introverted and mean
Thomas	Large, soft and cuddly
Waldo	Waldo?

As for the women:

Barbara	Fat but sexy
Emma	Pretty but silly
Florence	Masculine
Gillian	Pretty
Louise	Temperamental but likable
Maureen	Sultry and surly
Nancy	Spiteful
Pamela	Hard, ambitious and domineering
Patricia	Plain
Sally	Childish
Sarah	Sensual and selfish
Yolanda	Married to Waldo

Another of my favorites is a neat little pocket piece titled *Never Name the Baby Bill.* A self-professed rare collection of distinctive baby names, it hints at the charm and nuance of a veritable cornucopia of interesting possibilities from Arabella to Zachary. I mentioned it to a listener (who was actually calling from her hospital labor room) one morning when my friend John Gary was with me in the studio. Incidentally, I think that is the only "my friend the celebrity" line in this book. It was not used for effect. I happen to be a friend of John Gary's. I shall remain so no matter how often his voice changes. Anyhow, John heard me telling the mother-to-be about this book and he let out a squeal (this was way back when he was still a tenor). His wife, he excitedly informed me, was also about to deliver, and they were feverishly searching for a unique, distinctive name. *Never Name the*

PS. I threw in Waldo and Yolanda myself. They're made for each other.

Baby Bill—with entries such as Jago, Dalton, Cummings, and dozens more—sounded like the perfect answer to their dilemma. He was so enthused, I gave him my copy of the book. You would have thought it contained the formula for bathtub plutonium, he was so appreciative. Smell something coming? You always have had great sensors. A month or so later, the Garys had a baby boy. The unique, distinctive name they gave him was William. True story.

Far be it from me to start throwing stones. My youngest daughter, along with a few hundred thousand other beautiful people born during the seventies, is named Jennifer. What must seem like three million pages ago, I indicated that Jennifer and Michael are the current favorite American names. Mike has always been up near the top of the list, but Jennifer—like Kimberly, Michelle, and several other currently very popular names—is a late bloomer. Jennifer Jones, the actress; "Jennifer Juniper," Donovan's international hit record; and Jenny, the tear-jerking heroine of *Love Story* at work, I suppose. Regardless of the trigger, Jennifer is definitely on top today. As an indication of how popular she is, consider this: two out of every five girls and three out of every five boys born in this country are given one of the ten most popular names of the time. The current leaders, according to appropriately official-looking charts contained in *First Name First* by Leslie Alan Dunkling, are:

Girls	Boys
1. Jennifer	Michael
2. Amy	Jason
3. Sarah	Matthew
4. Michelle	Brian

5.	Kimberly	Christopher
6.	Heather	David
7.	Rebecca	John
8.	Catherine	James
9.	Kelly	Jeffrey
10.	Elizabeth	Daniel

Tie any one of those to a surname like Smith or Johnson and you will certainly be doing your part to make life miserable for the roll callers of tomorrow. Smith and Johnson, by the way, are easily the most common last names in America. Williams, Brown, Jones, Miller, Davis, Wilson, Anderson, and Taylor round out the top ten. Know number eleven? I'll give you some help. There are more Cohens than Smiths listed in the New York City phone book; Landry and Boudreau are both very big in New Orleans; and Boston has guzillions of Sullivans, Murphys, and McCarthys. These names, however, are a long way down the list. It isn't Carter. Even Phillips, in thirty-sixth place, nudges out the president and his kin. Poor old McNulty and Hicks aren't even close. They compete for last place on a roster of the top 2,000. Lewis and Clark show up in the low teens. Give up? Moore. Isn't that a terrific piece of information? Use it as you will, without charge or obligation.

Which combination do you think prevails world-wide—Michael Smith or Jennifer Johnson? Neither does. The single most common first name in the world is Mohammed, and there are more Wongs than Smiths, Johnsons, and Moores combined. Somewhere out there is a guy named Mohammed Michael Wong who is related to everybody. I'll pay a $100 finders fee to anyone who can get me his phone number.

Little Known Fact

If Wendy Hiller married the old baseballer Wally Moon, divorced him and married Perry Como, did it again with Giuseppi Verdi, and then Yves Montand, she'd be Wendy-Moon-Como-Verdi-Montand.

Before you allow all this nonsense to go to your head and decide to open a limited-production belt buckle factory, consider the odds against any first name staying on top for very long. They're not good. With the exception of the indomitable John, hot names come and go with faddish regularity. Barbara, for example, was number six on the girls' list twenty-five years ago, and Heather wasn't even in the top fifty. Today, Heather is number six, and Barbara is nowhere to be found. Remember, too, that Alexander, Edith, and Mildred were all once very big. If trends continue, Mary and Walter will be the next to go. I have a rough bulletin for you as well, George. You are definitely no longer in.

Glittery rock star David Bowie (David? For a glittery ac/dc rock star? All wrong!) Sure didn't force *his* son to settle for someone else's name. He picked something timeless, fad-proof and, in character, slightly bizarre: Zowie. Yep, Zowie Bowie. Personally, I think it is a lot of hooey, but individuality obviously counts big with the amplification set. David's close friends Tiny Tim, Frank Zappa, and Gracie Slick (since show biz types are always so chummy on *The Tonight Show*, I assume them all to be close friends) chose Tulip, Moon Unit, and god for their respective offspring.

God? No, god. Once you get past the shock of it, that one makes some sense. It has an unquestionable ring of authority, is easy to pronounce, and its potential contributions to the little Slick's success are enormous. Think how easy it would be to sell life insurance, for example, if you could tell prospective clients that god was calling. Develop a knack for impersonating George Burns and you'd really have it hammered.

The straight arrow lifestyle was evidently too much for spaced-out Gracie to abide. At last week's *Rolling Stone* press deadline, little god was rumored to be answering to China instead. Now that we two super powers seem to be such good buddies again, she'll probably re-re-name the kid Darth Vader or give it a set of catchy initials like V.D. Gracie is a real class act.

One final note regarding the name selection process. Don't worry about paying homage to your rich relatives. That's what middle names are for.

Hey, wait a minute. Time out! You almost let me forget about Rodrigo. He discovered America. His boss got all the credit but eagle-eye Rod was the lookout who actually spotted land first at about 2 A.M. on 12 October 1492. Considering he had imbibed his daily ration of two-thirds of a gallon of red wine, that was probably no simple task. So why is he such a stranger? Why aren't there any Rodrigo de Triana Day Parades or Trianavilles? Basic—he blew it. If the guy had only gotten some good advice and changed his name to Travolta. . . .

Question: What do Christopher Columbus, Paul Anka, Sally Rand, James Madison, and Henry Winkler have in common?

Answer: All of them belong or belonged to the group controversially immortalized by Randy Newman. Just a short reminder.

The Third Toughest Mystery Of All Time

When Johnny was four years old, he was sent on a train journey. Having made all the arrangements, a kindly, middle-aged man put him on the train and entrusted him to the care of the authorities. There was no accident, Johnny was in perfect health, and the authorities did all they could. But Johnny never arrived at his destination. How come?

Answer: Johnny was a goat. He ate his tags. Since no one could figure out where he was supposed to be going, where he wound up is anyone's guess.

94

A Flat Statement

The no-bra look will not catch on
At least that's my impression.
For if it does, gals built like me
Will suffer deep depression!
      Mary Knorowski
      (a regular listener, as though you couldn't
      tell)

Do You Recognize This Person?

She is the most beautiful girl in the world. At least that was the consensus of a group of international students who responded to a Lausanne University survey in the late 1960s.

As her composite picture may or may not make perfectly clear, her ideal features include: an English complexion, an Irish smile, French curves, a Spanish walk, Italian hair, Egyptian eyes, a Greek nose, American teeth, a Viennese voice, a Japanese laugh (difficult to capture in a mug shot), a Thai neck (should have been Thai thighs and a Czech neck, if you ask me), Argentine shoulders, Swiss hands, Scandinavian legs, Chinese feet, and an Australian bosom.

The poll's findings went on to recommend that she cook like a Frenchwoman, keep house like a German, be as docile as an Oriental, and dress as smartly as an American. An adequate package, I suppose.

Don't get uptight if this particular combination of pulchritudinous ingredients doesn't ring your chimes. That would only make you even with more than 97.2 percent of the world's population who didn't happen to be students in the vicinity of Lausanne University in the late 1960s. I believe the operative dreadful cliche reads "Beauty is in the eye of the beholder."

Did you notice my sophisticated put-down of cliches? I don't know exactly what it is that makes cliches so dreadful, but it is difficult, if not impossible, to sound witty and urbane without referring to them in such terms a minimum of twice per social encounter. In accordance with the mandate of the Fairness Doctrine (more radio talk), I hasten to add that the simple truth about cliches is that they are first and foremost simple truths.* That is why they are repeated often enough to become cliches.

The one concerning subjectivity of the beholder is substantiated by the abundance of wart hogs, manatees, and Gila monsters that Marlin Perkins has been chasing around all these years. Legend and history lend it credence as well. Helen of Troy, Cleopatra, Sleeping Beauty, Marilyn Monroe, Mary Queen of Scots, Brigitte Bardot, and innumerable other reigning super beauties have had their admiring legions. No two have looked alike.

Hair is supposedly the first thing that men notice. That's a likely story. Even if true, it wouldn't explain anything. Ranking heart-throbs have come with blonde, brunette, red, and occasionally mixed-flavor toppings. Even Ilia, the new navigator for the starship *Enterprise*, is building a devout corps of Trekkies, and she is completely bald.

Nor is magnetic allure any more consistent below the

* Except, perhaps, those concerning women drivers. Janet Guthrie seems to move around pretty well. I wonder if she's ever been to Memphis? It's illegal there for a woman to drive unless her car is preceded by a man running and waving a red flag to warn approaching motorists and pedestrians.

scalp. The all-time classic beauty, Venus de Milo, has a pug nose, no arms, and proportions ample enough to flop off the edges of any centerfold most men have pretended not to notice amidst the interesting articles and ads. Yet even she would shrink to Twiggy size next to a few of *Mondo Cane*'s featured attractions. Do you remember that thing? It was, for lack of a better term, a 1950s documentary which explored several of the world's most striking oddities. "A forerunner of new wave cinema-grotesque" one memorable advertisement teased with uncharacteristically complete integrity. One of the film's oddest oddities scanned an aboriginal tribe whose women were forced to sit in cramped cages and eat. There was nothing punitive involved; in their men's eyes, fat was where it was at. So these 350 pound and up debs just sat there and ate and ate and ate.

If this country harbored such extravagant tastes, three Miss Americas would have to wiggle into the same string bikini to get a whistle. The ostensible epitome of American femininity, Miss America's composite vitals from 1921 to date show her to be a 5′5″ tall blonde or brunette (pageant officials are rumored to consider redheads too likely to be swingers) who weighs 123 pounds and has a 34½″ bustline—a real Ziegfeld girl. Oh, come on now, don't tell me you've never heard of the "Ziegfeld Follies." No one is *that* young.

Florenz Ziegfeld's measurements for the ideal female figure were: neck, 12″; upper arm, 9½″ (how's that for attention to detail); bust, 34″; waist, 24″; wrist, 6″; hips, 34″; thigh, 19½″ (sorry, Raquel); calf, 13½″; ankle, 8″; height, 5′6¼″; and weight, 128 pounds. Those preferences say something profound about his personality, but to find out what, you'll have to give Nancy Hirschberg a call.

Nancy teaches psychology at the University of Illinois Circle Campus. Her specialty is body research. Ms. Hirschberg's major hypothesis is that men reveal their characters by the part or parts of a woman's body they like best. Men who prefer girls with big breasts, for example, are likely to date frequently, say witty things, and drink and smoke, which indicates why Dolly Parton's suitors are such total wrecks. Those who prefer small-breasted women tend to hold traditional religious beliefs, be mildly depressed, and drink less than others. Guys who dig women with big hips are guilty, self-abasing, and socially dependent. Those who favor long-legged girls are not very aggressive and drink little, while the ones who choose short-legged females generally enjoy social activities. I don't know what the story is on Mademoiselle Polaire's fans. She was, and still is for all I know, a Guinness record-holding French actress with a 13" waistline. Do you believe that? Most people have necks bigger than thirteen inches around. Why some people even have . . . well, never mind.

No academic conclusions regarding men's preferences in female neck, upper arm, or wrist proportions have yet been made public, but one fact seems clear—Flo Ziegfeld was a man ahead of his time. His chorus of would-be starlets dwarfed their contemporaries, but make today's 5'5", 127 pound, 33.9"-busted average American girl look like a virtual clone. A successful ladies' man named Flo had to have something going for him.

I wonder what Flo would have thought of the girl from Lausanne. In this lascivious beholder's opinion she is a definite keeper, but nowhere near perfect. Even if the survey's respondents had been connoisseurs enough to have given her a black's back, Polish lips, and Portuguese knees, there is no way she could have been. Although, as

100

anyone with eyes can plainly see, Sophia comes very close (not close enough, of course) no one person can realistically be expected to possess all of everyone's favorite attributes. I speak with utter infallibility on this point because I happen to know a guy who thinks Phyllis Diller is an absolute knockout. Of course, he is too bombed most of the time to know any better.

Maybe all those bright young students from around the world who got together on that Swiss hilltop to cast their ballots and sing Coca-Cola jingles should have saved themselves the trouble. Perhaps they thought they had been asked to describe the most beautiful north-European girl in the world. If not, they're all budding Foster Brooks protégés.

I don't mean to imply he's a ten percenter, but if we ever asked Foster to play a game of leap year roulette with us he'd probably ask for a date with the one in the heart because that was the direction he was tilting at the moment.

Every leap year Foster (no relation) and Kleiser, the major outdoor advertising company, gives us a scattering of large billboards to fill with the names and descrip-

WALLY PHILLIPS
591-4090

KATHY, 27, Kikky Capricorn
JOANNIE, 22, Sports & Spice
MICKEY, 26, 40/24/34
URSULA, 24, Classy Import
PEGGY, 27, BS + MS & Beautiful

FOSTER and KLEISER

tive sizzle of some all-girl girls who are ready, willing, and able to turn the tables on tradition. Available applicants volunteer for the assignment on the air, write their own copylines, then wait for bids from ardent would-be suitors to come rolling in. And roll in they do, by the ton. Okay, by the big mail bag.*

Is this billboard routine another tacky, demeaning expression of our sick society? I know of three young couples who sure don't think so. They're married today, happily I hope, precisely because they were willing to take a good-natured poke at hallowed double standards. Their results were far more dramatic than any we expected when you originally suggested the idea. In the beginning, it was just a tongue-in-cheek alternative to Sadie Hawkins' Day racing prompted by that old Judy Holliday movie.

I don't know if any damsel featured on the board above got a Prince Charming out of the deal, but I do know who got the most mail. Care to take a stab? A possible explanation can be found in the "googol" chapter. Sounds like a pretty good chapter, doesn't it? Of course, early impressions can be deceiving.

Perfection in the female of the species has, of course, been the subject of heated debate ever since males first learned how to ogle. Overt man watching is a relatively recent development. Its number one proponent is Suzy Mallery, the Happy Looker, whose Man Watchers Incorporated publishes an annual list of the Ten Men Most Worth Watching. Early perennials Paul Newman and Robert Redford have been replaced by such disparate sex objects as Arnold Schwarzenegger, Ram quarterback Pat Hayden, and pudgy captain of the *Love Boat* Gavin Mac-

---

* Incidentally, a New York court has held that a strong desire to marry on the part of a man is not prima facie evidence of insanity.

With his own enormously successful syndicated daily program and regular feature segment on the Today Show, *Phil Donahue* (the one on the left) is the hottest thing in TV. He deserves to be. He's good. Very good. So good that he was named first runner-up on Suzy's list of "almosts" last year. I, for one, find the combination of all that talent and all that hulk in one package more than a bit offensive.

Leod. Robert Urich of *Vegas* made it in '79. That comes as
no surprise here. Bob used to sell commercials for WGN
Radio. It's a good thing he quit when he did. We were
losing about three secretaries and who knows how many
upper level executives a week to heat prostration for a
while there. Our medical insurance rates were about to
go up.

Suzy says the qualifications for making the list include
charm, wit, facial features, popularity, personality, taste
in clothing, and contributions to society, but "what really counts is the body." This female chauvinism has
simply got to stop. What about our minds? Don't they
count for anything anymore?

The ultimate test of any opposite's appeal is probably
still the answer to the old question "With whom would
you most like to be stranded on a desert island?"

Men don't play the game very well. They just can't
stand the prosperity. Given a world full of prospective
castaways to choose from, they bounce all over the place
from Betty Grable to Cheryl Tiegs and all points in-
between. By implication, they would really like to be
stranded with a harem.

Talk is cheap. The vast majority of men, even those
macho studs with standard-issue moustaches and idiotic
spoon pendants, are actually intimidated by their Fantasy Island girls in the flesh. Telling evidence of this
phenomenon can be observed any night of the week at
your favorite neighborhood disco or singles bar. Leaving
the real foxes (chicks, for those of you past puberty) in
confused solitude, the young men seek out plain Janes
with whom the threat of rejection in those terrible seven
seconds it takes to get an answer is less awesome. This
does not please the beautiful wallflowers. Given their
druthers, they would just as soon have the opportunity to

This candid shot of femme fatale Ann Margaret and her newest rumored heart-throb is proof positive that not all men are intimidated by or become disoriented in the presence of outlandish beauty.

Despite the missing "s," TV's Lee Phillip and yours truly are occasionally mistaken for a twosome. She is too polite, refined, dignified, and charming to even consider publicly guffawing at the notion, but husband Bill Bell (the other handsome one) must have difficulty suppressing the urge. He's the creator and writer of the popular daytime drama The Young and the Restless, *so he probably has a few thousand sparky lines ready for any such absurd plot wrinkle. The young and the restless? You know, I love them both and consider them my two best friends, but I still haven't figured out which is which.*

do their own rejecting. Of course, some of the responsibility is theirs as well. I, for one, am forever volunteering to help resolve the injustice of it all, but to date, zero starlets or cover girls have taken me up on the offer. Explain women.

Oh, it really isn't germane to this discussion anyway. We were trying to figure out which "she" a typical "he" would invite to a desert island, not a dance floor. Man, men, that is one tough assignment. So tough that I can only recall one brother who ever came close to speaking for all of us with anything less than a sorority-sized guest list. He requested "a sexy lady doctor who grew up on a farm." He didn't happen to mention her ability to keep house like a German.

Women are much less fickle; they are absolutely predictable, in fact. We have repeatedly jumped in and out of this "what if" situation, and her reply has been "my gynecologist" every time. No wonder it is so difficult to get into medical school.

On yet another fascinating side of the physical attraction coin, it seems we don't even notice in our opposites the things we like least about ourselves. Either that, or noses, knees, and spare tires are too repugnant to mention in polite company. I am reasonably certain the former applies. While I don't pretend to be smart enough to understand what really makes us tick, there simply must be more to the equation than our instinctive fondness for each other's bulges. Don't get me wrong. I like a good-looking bulge or two as much as you do, just not so much that I measure worth by girth.

That, you are probably thinking with justifiable indignation, is the first non-sexist notion uttered in the last twelve pages. Sorry. My genuine respect and admiration for Helen Keller, Joan of Arc, Golda Meir, Madame Curie,

Margaret Mead, Frances Kelsey,* and many many more worthwhile human beings who happened to be women notwithstanding, a fact of nature is at work here. There are men who like women, women who like men, men who like men, women who like women, and then some people who run on alternating currents. Right or wrong, I am a man who likes women who like men. Don't pick on my hang-ups and I won't pick on yours.

Christian Nevell Bovee said it:
"Next to God, we are indebted to women, first for life itself, and then for making it worth having."

The guy who owns this thriving emporium isn't quite as eloquent, but his thought is no less sincere. . . .

* Frances Kelsey is, perhaps, my all-time favorite person of either gender. She was the FDA administrator chiefly responsible for banning thalidomide from distribution within the United States.

Too Much Can Blur Your Vision

Every so often, like during solar eclipses and on Sundays immediately preceding Gordon Macrae Film Festivals, I play a record on the radio. As soon as Willie Nelson's croaking or Barbra Streisand's exercises in nasal decongestion become as entertaining as a chat with you, I'll play more. Don't hold your breath.

Radio listeners are radio listeners for three basic reasons. Some want the sound of music or muzak or both to accompany their comings and goings. Others are looking for companionship and involvement. The remainder are after something specific and timely, usually news and information regarding the weather, traffic, sports scores and the like. That makes it tough to court universal appeal. Most radio stations don't even try. They pick a precise slice of the potential listening audience and play whatever they think those target listeners want to hear over and over and over. A few, with what I think are known in the trade as Adult Contemporary Personality Programming Formats take a shot by gabbing around the music of Harry Chapin and other message minstrels who simultaneously sing, stomp, strum, talk, and mumble about the foibles of everyday life. Designed to somehow push everyone's hot buttons, these sonic polyglots tend to be too diffuse to completely satisfy anyone. My efforts, on the other hand, are absolute marvels of goal-oriented cause and effect. Designed to appeal to no one in particular, they are enormously successful.

Happily, in the context of personal survival (my number one priority, just like yours), that isn't true, but I liked the line too well not to use it. Call it an irresistible urge, a compulsion, a space filler.

Paul Simon's "Fifty Ways To Leave Your Lover" is one record which we did give a few thousand twirls a while back. No payola or illicit compromise was involved. The tune was something of a groupy news event at the time, in that it was Simon's first post-Garfunkel hit. You did request it once or twice, and I figured, if I ever got lucky enough to have the problem, a couple of the lyric's sure-fire exit lines might come in handy.

Immediately seeing through my sudden and uncharacteristic reversion to big-time disc jockey status, someone's grandmother from Skokie called and advised, "You don't vant to learn how to leaf a girl. You vant to learn how to *find* a nise girl." Like all other grandmothers from Skokie or anywhere else, she was on the money. I'd already had two ill-fated trips down the aisle with the same lady. Not even the three most wonderful children in the world could help make it work. Strike three would be a crusher. My insecurity apparently hung out like William Claude Dunkenfield's proboscis. The switchboard was instantly a-twinkle with suggestions on how to be a great lover, not how not to be one. None have yet inspired Paul Simon to trigger a smash hit sequel, but a few of them were gang-buster material.

110

TOO MUCH CAN BLUR YOUR VISION

Twenty-six Ways to Lure a Lover

1. Tell her that anything she may have heard about you was exaggerated.
2. Once in a while, very quietly, take out the garbage.
3. Gasp with delight when she's cleaned the hall closet.
4. Admit your mother's cooking always gave you heartburn.
5. Tell her you never believed it could be like this.
6. Assure her the models and actresses you meet are shallow, cold, and much too skinny.
7. Bring her one rose. (Cheaper in tandem with the car pool.)
8. Nibble her ear while she's scrambling the eggs.
9. Carry her across the room, if you're both in shape.
10. Get jealous the day the repairman is coming.
11. Tell her she doesn't need any make up.
12. Buy her a string bikini.
13. Tell her you not only love her, you like her.
14. Get romantic in the middle of the afternoon.
15. Put the bigger half of the egg roll on her plate.
16. Tell her you love her while she's diapering the baby.
17. Send her a schmaltzy card on Columbus Day.
18. Call her baby, chérie, Cara Mia, pussycat, lamb chop, Sir or Ms., as your relationship warrants.
19. Tell her you couldn't make it without her.
20. Say they take after their mother whenever anyone tells you the children are beautiful.
21. Ask her to feed you chicken soup when you're sick.

22. Decide her mother is a sweet woman at heart. Buy her a string bikini too.
23. Growl when she calls you tiger.
24. Light two cigarettes at the same time. Give one to her. Try to look like that suave Frenchman on the late show.
25. Better yet, tell her you quit smoking as a gesture of affection for her. Tell her to quit too or you will turn on some Paul Simon albums.

Lest you Don Juans think an amorous refresher course unnecessary, consider a recent survey conducted by assistant professors at two southeastern universities. While the study drew no academic conclusions (I think only full professors are allowed to do that), it did come up with some interesting findings about what people like to do in their spare time. First choice for men was sex. (For this they needed a survey?) Women preferred reading books.* What's more, the longer they were married the more the women who responded to this survey liked to read. An invitation for emotional involvement on the most ethereal plane is evidently feeble competition to Tolstoy or Jacqueline Susann down in peanut country. The next time their belles stay curled up with a literary preventative for three or four months at a crack, some of those good ol' boys probably ought to give number twenty-six a try.

26. Mention the display of erotic paperbacks you saw in Kroch's & Brentano's window this afternoon.

* But don't despair, men; sex did beat out "sewing for leisure" by one percent in the ladies' vote.

Tell her the covers were so raunchy they made you blush.*

Whatever your tactics, I wish you well in the Battle of Separate But Equal. The end is worth the effort. As an American Greeting which someone once spent today's equivalent of two dollars plus postage (inflation is everywhere) to send me said:

- Love is finding the answer and losing sight of the question.
- Love is hell but more fun to make than war.
- Love is that which keeps a girl from noticing how short he is.
- Love is like running down the street naked. You can be forgiven for it on the grounds of temporary insanity.†
- Love is a word used in tennis by people who can't score any other way.
- Love is one of the things that causes babies, second only to carelessness.
- Love is the soy sauce on the chop suey of life.
- Love is like a mushroom. You never know whether it's the real thing until it's too late.

---

* Blush—a temporary erethism or a calorific affluengence of the physiognomy, ediologized by the perceptiveness of the censorium in a predicament of shame, anger, or other cause eventuating in the facial capillaries of the parasissis whereby . . . .

† This is only true west of the part of the country in which they call milkshakes *frappes* and pop *soda*.

The Second Toughest Mystery of All Time

(Elapsed solution time: 51 minutes, 36 seconds and two political debates.)

A very dark-skinned black man was walking along a country road. There was no moon, the road was not lighted, and he was dressed completely in black. An automobile came tearing around a bend at seventy miles an hour. Amazingly, it was able to come to a screeching halt a few yards away from the man, leaving him uninjured. How come?

Answer: It was broad daylight.

So You Want To Be a Pronouncer

My friend, you are in luck. The Wally Phillips Famous Announcers School for Budding Dance Contest Emcees and Other Misdirected Youth (WPFASBDCEOMY, for short) is now in session.

Did you know that the fast-paced, glamorous broadcast industry has a crying need for fresh new superstars? Well it does! Ed McMahon, Barbara Walters, and Gary Coleman aren't getting any younger you know.

This could be your opportunity of a lifetime!

Do you have what it takes?

The following radio and television personality aptitude test is scientifically designed to help you find out. You may take it without obligation of any kind. Simply pretend you are sitting before a microphone in the lavish studios of a major market radio or TV station and ad-lib endings for these authentic broadcast phrases.

1. "We'll be back in a moment after these important words from our _____." (srosnops)
2. "Due to technical difficulties beyond our _____." (lortnoc)

115

3. "The time in ten seconds will be ten o'clock. Time now for the ten o'clock ———————." (swen)

4. "Get down and ———————." (eigoob)

If your answers match those cleverly concealed by our professional faculty of famous announcer, or if they can be found in any English language dictionary, you qualify.

Congratulations! Broadcasting is definitely your field! Now, to get started on your personalized formal training program simply—

1. Place $50,000 in unmarked, small denomination bills in a plain brown envelope and send it to my attention. Be sure to act today!

2. Practice signing your autograph and smiling. (Doing this in front of a full-length mirror will help you polish these most necessary skills.)

3. Be prepared to read the following sample audition script in one minute or less when we call:

UNDER THE KLIEG LIGHTS, THE HARASSED RADIO ANNOUNCER CORRUGATED HIS FOREHEAD, COGITATING ON THE VAGARIES OF ENGLISH ORTHOEPY AND PHONEMIC EXTRAVAGANCES. HE FEARED IGNOMINY. "UGH," HE OPINED, SOTTO VOCE, "ONLY AN ANCIENT CURATOR OF SOME OTIOSE AND SACRELIGIOUS ATHENAEUM OR PERHAPS A PERAMBULATING ENCYCLOPEDIA COULD MAKE PROGRESS WITH THIS HEINOUS PALIMPSEST. HOW I WISH I MIGHT HAVE BEEN EITHER A DOUR IGNORAMUS OR AN IMPIOUS CABALLERO WATCHING A ROBUSTIOUS MELEE! BETTER EVEN A FLACCID TYMPANIST IN THE HAREM OF SOME ESOTERIC MAHARAJA OR RECONDITE BLACKGUARD NOURISHED ON RATIONED OLEOMARGARINE THAN TO BE CONCOCTING BROMIDIC CLICHES AT THE INANE COMMANDS OF YONDER GRISLY PANJANDRUM." AGAIN HE MUSED,

"THESE LARYNGEAL EFFULGENCES ARE, I SUPPOSE, THE **SINE QUA NON** OF ETHEREAL BROADCASTING. BUT I'D MUCH RATHER SPEAK AD LIBITUM." ALAS, HIS GARRULITIES—UNRAVELED AD INFINITUM— WERE SUPERFLUOUS. AFTER ALL, HE WAS A WELL PAID STAFF JANISSARY ASSIGNED TO AN AESTHETIC PROGRAM. AS THE DIRECTOR'S AGED, ASCETIC FINGER BECKONED, OUR HERO ACCEDED TO THE DEMANDS OF THE OCCASION AND LUXURIATED IN THE LUSH VERBIAGE OF APOTHEGMS, WITH A MACHINATION HERE AND A PRONUNCIAMENTO THERE, SIEVED FROM YON SPONSOR'S LONG-LOVED BROCHURE.

HOURS LATER, WHEN THE AMPLIFICATOR WAS QUIESCENT, HE ADDRESSED AN INQUIRY TO HIS LIN- GUALLY ACERB SPOUSE WHO, BY WAY OF ASIDE, WAS WEARING A FUCHSIA BLOUSE DECOLLETE IN SEPULCHRAL OROTUNDITIES. "I ASK YOU, O MELLIF- LUOUS ONE, DID I ERR PHONETICALLY THIS EVE- NING?" TO WHICH SHE REPLIED DYSPHONICALLY, "NO, MY HIRSUTE KNIGHT," PANICULATED, AND FELL INTO THE ARMS OF MORPHEUS. LATER, WHEN LESLIE—THAT WAS THE UXORIOUS ANNOUNCER'S PATRONYMIC—DREAMED OF AN UBIQUITOUS, MONOSYLLABIC PATOIS, A BEAUTIFUL SMILE HOV- ERED OVER HIS WIZENED PHYSIOGNOMY. THUS, HE WAS FOUND STERTORING LONG AFTER OLD SOL HAD CROSSED THE HORIZON.

Well done! You are such a natural I am amazed no major market producer has discovered you long before now. No matter. You are now officially ready to begin your exciting new high paying career in electronic show biz. Sure hope you can find a job.

And speaking of hope (clever transition lines are essential to a star's repertoire), this nice young broadcast hopeful just showed up hat in hand and personally delivered his plain brown envelope. A nice touch. I wonder what ever became of him?

The Language Lesson #2

K.I.S.S. (Keep It Simple, Stupid)

The preceding gobbledegook audition is real. It has sabotaged more pompous self-professed major talents than laryngitis and bad ratings combined. Alliteration and discordant rhyme are two of the prime ingredients in its nasty mix.

Tongue-twisters like "red Buick, blue Buick, red leather, yellow leather"; "The sixth sick sheik's sixth sheep's sick" (which Guinness says is toughest to date); and the ever-popular convoluted conversation between a woman and her plumber:

"Are you copper-bottoming 'em, my man?"

"No, mum, I'm aluminuming 'em, mum."

are fine for woeful out-of-work wordsmiths and plurality-pursuing politicians prone to calcifying constituents' comprehension. If, however, you'd rather be understood, don't use too many similar sounds in sequence.

Orange, silver, and intellectual are recommended as habit-breakers. They are among the most difficult words in the English language to rhyme and overuse. Were it not for the efforts of a few geniuses like Stephen Sondheim, they might be impossible. His unappreciated helpful hint is:

> To find a rhyme for silver
> Or any rhymeless rhyme
> Requires only will, ver-
> bosity and time.

Thanks a bunch, Steve.

OO–
SCREEEECH
YOU
OH CAN
SAY

Probably not.

A leading bass-baritone of the Metropolitan Opera Company and musical administrator of the John F. Kennedy Center for the Performing Arts, George London said in a *Life* magazine music review that our national anthem, "The Star-Spangled Banner," is ". . . just too hard. It covers a range of an octave and five tones, far too great for the average untrained voice . . . is awkwardly constructed . . . has hazy lyrics, and is generally avoided like the plague by most singers who care about their reputations."

Do you think such blasphemous rhetoric indicates pinko leanings? Julie Rosegrant sure doesn't. Julie, a seventy-plus grandmother from Putney, Vermont, heads a radical organization dedicated to the outlandish proposition that a country's theme song should be something its citizens can sing. The real, undoubtedly subversive mission of the group is probably either unknown or classified information somewhere in Washington. Knowing our peerless leaders, I would guess it is classified under "Unknown."

I met comrade—I mean Mrs. Rosegrant the same way I have met most other people worth meeting over the years. You introduced us. It was on the morning after some major athletic event at which the pre-game ceremonial dirge had been played in an even more impossible to reach than usual key. The crowd will usually rise on command, shuffle uncomfortably, pretend earnest participation, and really blast ". . . and the home of the brave." But this organist was so far out of whack that, by the time the bombs started bursting in midair, everyone in the place had caught the infectious giggles. I have never had the good fortune to watch thousands of people simultaneously giggle, but it must be quite a sight. The phones were ablaze.

"An outrage!" stormed one Howard Miller impersonator.

"Absolutely shocking," echoed Maude Frickert.

"Far out," added another, ambivalently.

When words like "conspiracy" and "plot" began flying around, I knew it was time to set the crack investigating team of my producer and most-valued accomplice, Marilyn Miller, and her magic control room phone to work on the case. In no time they had tracked down an informant from the game site's management. He was in the shower.* He tried to dismiss the problem as a symptom of the organ's imminent electronic mid-life crisis, apologized for having been party to such an affront to

* Men generally prefer taking showers because the acoustical qualities of a ceramic closet make them sound so macho when they sing. Female voices, on the other chord, tend to become rather shrill when bounced off walls, so women almost universally tub bathe in silence. They sing while driving—even in Memphis.

everyone's patriotic sensibilities, and assured Marilyn that the team would soon win a game. Thinking fast, he then suggested she call the organist for her side of the story.

"That's ridiculous," one of the other party's precinct captains chuckled before we got any further. "I was there too. No one was being intentionally disrespectful to the flag. The 'Star-Spangled Banner' is always impossible to sing. Last night it was also implausible, and that struck everyone as funny."*

Such hot debates tend to ebb and flow, so the ensuing flurry of opinions agreed that the incident was being overplayed. Finally, someone suggested that we put the question in perspective by chatting with this nice old lady out East. It turned out to be one of my everlasting favorite suggestions.

After considering the evidence, Mrs. R. said it didn't sound to her like it had been the organist's or the organ's or even the crowd's fault. She thought it was Ralph Tomlinson's fault. Ralph, I learned, was the distinguished and no doubt well-intentioned, albeit tone-deaf senator who spearheaded the song's adoption as our official tune back in 1931. Yep, 1931. Bet you thought the forefathers had jumped right up, doffed their deodorant wigs, and belted a few bars of the thing immediately after signing the Declaration of Independence. Wrong. Chiseled in granite this tradition is not.

Oh, the melody had been belted plenty during the revolutionary period, all right—but by the other team. It was an old English drinking song known popularly as "The Olde Tin Roof" and academically as "The Anac-

---

* The organist was definitely not Nancy Faust. Anyone who would laugh at her is both tone-deaf and blind. Maybe she's what Ralph had in mind. Think she'd like to become our national organist?

reontic Song" or "To Anacreon In Heaven." For my self-ish purposes, it would have been a happy coincidence if that strange word "anacreontic" had proved derivative of "anachronistic." Can't win 'em all. But according to Webster's Third New International Dictionary (the big, fat, unabridged baby), anacreontic simply means a drinking song or light lyric. In Greek prosody, whatever that is, it unsimply means, "a verse having the cadence analyzed as two ionics *a minore* with anaclasis and sup-plement, or as iambic dimeter catalectic with anapestic opening." Of course, you probably knew that all along.

The hallowed words (which a *Cleveland Press* Bi-centennial Editorial calling for the anthem's repeal said, "Not one loyal American in 10,000 can recite—let alone sing") were written about a relatively minor incident during an entirely different war in 1814.

Quick, recite a stanza of "The Star-Spangled Banner."

So you happen to be the one in 10,000. Big deal. Want a medal? Now try the second stanza. How about the third? Bet you've never even heard the fourth. It goes like this:

> And where is that band who so vauntingly swore
> That the havoc of war and the battle's confusion
> A home and a country should leave us no more?
> Their blood has washed out their foul footsteps'
> pollution.
> No refuge could save the hireling and slave
> From the terror of flight, or the gloom of the
> grave;
> And the Star-Spangled Banner in triumph doth
> wave
> O'er the land of the free and the home of the
> brave!

Hah! I tricked you. That was the third stanza. Touching sentiment though, isn't it? I would particularly enjoy a chance to warble that part about the foul footsteps' pollution sometime.

I am not, by the way, off on this diatribe because the song lacks historical (I really think that should read "ourstorical") value. Renewed popularity in the wake of changing times, or revamped style and treatment is no indictment. It is a compliment, and really rather common. As evidence, consider the *Readers' Digest*'s successful albums full of musical re-treads that had originally flopped.

The Beatles' classic "Yesterday" was once called "Scrambled Eggs." Tony Bennett's career-saver, "I Left My Heart in San Francisco," was introduced with totally different lyrics to a militantly disinterested public back in 1954 by an operatic contralto named Claramae Turner. Roger Williams's famous instrumental version of "Autumn Leaves," which sold more than 2.5 million copies, was the unlikely offspring of an old French poem. Getting music from a pile of words has always sounded a little like designing space shuttles by looking at canoes, but it obviously worked for Roger and has, in varying degrees, for several other musical better mousetrap builders.

A few more intriguing musical oddities don't really fit here, so I'll throw them in just to be cantankerous.

"When I go to sleep, I never count sheep . . . I count all the charms about Linda"—these beginning lines of a big hit of the forties were written and sung by Jack Lawrence about his lawyer's young daughter who is now a popular singer in her own right and the wife of a left-handed

British pop balladeer with a sinus disorder that made him and his amply-frocked friends millionaires. Know who she was and is?

If you said Jane Barbe, you lose. Good guess though. The ingenue honoree was none other than Linda Eastman McCartney. As I said, Jane Barbe was a really good guess, except for the difference in the name and the fact that she lives in Georgia and isn't wed to an ex-Beatle. After all, she is the single most often heard recording artist in the world. Millions listen to her dulcet tones every day. Jane, for the benefit of you few who don't keep up with the times, is the voice of most of the phone company's recorded announcements. How's that for exposure?

As she might have said if I had thought to ask, "The time at the tone will be time to get back to the subject, *doooooooooooooooooooooooooooooooooooooooooooooooooooooo*

Even the most frequently sung English language song in the entire world was originally called "Good Morning To You." Incidentally, the rights to the tune are still owned by the estate of the two New York ladies who penned it. All of you birthday kids (10 million of you a day at last count) who have been bellowing it while blowing out party candles and getting your germs all over the cake for all these years are building up some pretty terrific royalty bills. You could lose the deed to the ranch if they ever decide to start collecting. Oh, a rare flash of brilliance. Maybe we should make "Happy Birthday" our national anthem. It's easy to sing, an upper, and would go great with the big tri-centennial celebration the Madison Avenue folks are no doubt already planning. (This is an unconfirmed rumor, but I understand they are trying to arrange to have old satellites from every nation crash into New York Harbor the next time around. It's going to be called the arrival of the Tall Blips. Keep that under your hat until the announcement, will you?) The song was even written in this country. Perfect. Shall we start a petition? How about a write-in campaign? A chain letter?

Please don't misunderstand. I don't mind the idea of having a national anthem. Precisely the opposite, in fact. It would just be so much nicer if ours sounded more like something else. Something like "America the Beautiful," "My Country 'tis of Thee," or "The Battle Hymn of the Republic" instead of a dentist's drill. The words to all three of those essentially American songs have strength, dignity, and charm. Their melodies almost sing themselves. They make sense. That may be the problem.

If that isn't the hang-up, it must be the fact that all three of them have the same problem as Kate Smith's favorite show-stopper. They all have a sort of, well, y'know, I mean, uh...are there any kids in the room?...uh, well a kind of religious sound to them. There, I said it! Religion! That took plenty of editorial integrity and sheer guts I'll have you know. See, it doesn't matter that ninety-four percent of us believe in something or other up there out there somewhere. It doesn't matter that two percent are ambivalent and another two percent don't even know what we're talking about. What matters is the remaining two percent who so adamantly believe in nothing but now. They've had schools that allow or don't allow prayers in and out of the headlines not to mention the courts for years. This two percent has had educators so spooked that they apparently haven't been able to teach much reading lately. Powerful folks, atheists. So powerful that I shudder to think of what they may now do to me. A ban on radio in public places does not appeal.

Neither does the Star-Spangled Banner. I think I'll risk the former to get rid of the latter. At the risk of redundant risk, I join Julie and her fellow Putneyites in suggesting that having a song you can't sing as your national anthem is first and foremost basically dumb.

So what are we going to do about it? Very probably, very little. We could but we won't. Tax revolts and Mrs. Mayor notwithstanding, we are a pretty apathetic bunch most of the time. Never was that more clearly illustrated than the day a few years back when radio station WCLS in Columbus, Georgia dedicated an entire four-hour talk show to the subject of public apathy. They had three calls.

Patriotic Pop Quiz

Name a popular spectator sport that somehow suc-
ceeds without fife & drum pre-game rituals.

Here's a clue.

Here's another.

The answer is bowling, but I couldn't find any cutesy pictures of me not being able to do that. Besides, these perfect golf shot shots allow me to acknowledge the way-above-and-beyond-the-call contributions of some legitimate giants of the species.

I am sure that Jack Nicklaus, Arnold Palmer, Lee Trevino, and even Glenn Campbell play benefit rounds for charity all the time. I am equally sure, however, that they are seldom forced to do so with a silly looking duffer in tow. That they have all done so with grace, charm, wit, and me at one time or another (Grace, Charm, and Wit aren't too bad, but I can't hit the thing straight for the life of me) qualifies every one of them for some kind of special citation in the Big Heart department.

My ro (I can't refer to it as a round because it was mercifully rained-out after four holes) with Jack Nicklaus is the one that really stands out. He was literally a last-second replacement for an ailing super-Mexican who thoroughly humiliated me at a later date. Jack had won a tourney hundreds of miles away the day before. He was tired, harried, and probably didn't have any idea who this nut in the funny suit was.

He was also as warm and personable as any man I have ever met.

He was also, also something of a subtler Don Rickles. I'll never forget that first tee. If you have played the game you know the first tee is a horrendous experience under any circumstances. I mean, you could be playing alone at four in the morning and still know some squirrels were cracking-up from watching your stance. Before a gallery of people who have payed real money for the questionable privilege, and in the company of three guys who hit the ball a thousand yards as straight as an arrow without taking the socks off of their clubs, it is absolutely bloodcurdling, Needless to say, I darned near killed a spectator with my inaugural shank of the day. Lucky thing for him I can't hit it hard, it could have been a very uncomfortable moment. Anyway, the crowd fell silent. The victim watched his life flash by. Glenn started humming "Houston" or some other song about a city.* A couple of squirrels began giggling in a nearby tree. Jack just smiled and stage-whispered, "Don't get to play too much, do you?" He then very quietly and sincerely offered to help with my game. Can you imagine that? You get probably the best golfer in history out of bed at three in the morning and ask him to fly to a strange town to play golf with a goof, and he offers a free lesson. All I know is that if that guy ever needs help with his wardrobe or anything else at which I excel, he can count on me.

* All Glenn Campbell songs are about cities.

Your Death Date

The ability to foretell such a dubious occasion should logically be in about as much demand as a talent for backing up sewers. So much for logic. What began as an offhand mention of an insurance table has now Frank-ensteined to the point where hardly a day (okay, hardly a week) goes by without someone calling to ask for his or her punctuation date. It is either some kind of macabre mass obsession or a sneaky way of getting a fix on when to start straightening out one's act. My hunch is the latter.

"See, it's like this, St. Peter. Sure, I was a wild and crazy guy back in the old days, but lately I have been an absolute model of decorum, a real narrow arrow, definite harp and wings material."

That sort of reformed prodigal routine is rumored to play very well upstairs, but it won't be too easy to use unless you know when "lately" is going to be. If you don't know, you may have to start being good long before it is necessary. For heaven's sake, our economy is in enough trouble already. Can you imagine what a sudden epidemic of rampant niceness and good might do to it? On this basis alone the service is worthwhile. The execution (no pun intended) is, however, getting a tad cumbersome. All the math involved is just too time-consuming for someone who burns out as many pocket calculators with built-in lifetime batteries as I do. What's more, sigh, I don't have quite as much time left as most of you. The somber fact is that you will have to watch Guy Lombardo's great-grand-nephew and his sophisticated friends celebrate the turn of the century at the Waldorf on your hologram viewing panel without me. By then, I shall have been wherever I shall be for 228 days.

That's okay. Have a nice time anyway. I'll give your best to Guy if I bump into him.

Call me if you must, but I would frankly prefer that you figure out your own departure schedule from here on out. It isn't difficult. First, find your age as of your last birthday in either of the following mortality table's outside columns. Check your adjacent expected number of years and days to live. Using the chart which follows the chart which follows, add them to your last birthdate. Set aside the last two or three weeks for insufferably good behavior and you have it made. If, by the way, you don't like the way this deal works out, blame Jim Halas or any other friendly State Farm agent you happen to know. It's their chart.

Complete Expectation of Life

left to go

	Male (yrs/days)	Female (yrs/days)
5	71/252	76/364
6	70/254	76/4
7	69/261	75/7
8	68/264	74/11
9	67/273	73/15
10	66/307	72/17
11	65/314	71/20
12	64/316	70/24
13	63/329	69/28
14	62/341	68/32
15	61/359	67/39
16	60/364	66/43
17	60/6	65/46
18	59/8	64/54
19	58/10	63/57
20	57/37	62/64
21	56/41	61/67
22	55/50	60/75
23	54/53	59/78
24	53/84	58/89
25	52/90	57/96
26	51/94	56/103
27	50/100	55/100
28	49/100	54/116
29	48/112	53/126

30	47/138	52/130
31	46/212	51/140
32	45/182	50/147
33	44/187	49/160
34	33/190	48/170
35	42/206	47/180
36	41/209	46/191
37	40/264	45/201
38	39/270	44/204
39	38/291	43/217
40	37/320	42/244
41	36/358	41/259
42	36/6	40/270
43	35/14	39/281
44	34/28	38/312
45	33/106	37/330
46	32/124	36/348
47	31/162	36/4
48	30/201	35/21
49	29/241	34/46
50	28/313	33/67
51	27/364	32/92
52	27/54	31/121
53	26/112	30/151
54	25/181	29/180
55	24/256	28/207
56	23/334	28/8
57	23/96	26/290
58	22/126	25/351
59	21/188	25/35
60	20/292	24/89
61	20/28	23/143
62	19/123	22/200
63	18/207	21/262

64	17/327	20/338
65	17/61	20/35
66	16/167	19/103
67	15/273	18/167
68	15/32	17/241
69	14/147	16/320
70	13/270	16/28
71	13/39	15/104
72	12/160	14/190
73	11/303	13/278
74	11/92	13/17
75	10/67	12/123
76	10/35	11/217
77	9/106	10/354
78	8/4	10/116
79	8/177	9/232
80	7/171	9/28
81	7/180	8/176
82	7/17	7/343
83	6/204	7/144
84	6/58	6/330
85	5/267	6/150
86	5/123	5/364
87	4/347	5/125
88	4/113	5/91
89	4/75	4/303
90	3/307	4/194
91	3/106	4/99
92	3/92	4/15

93 and up . . . you still have plenty of time to make a killing doing yogurt commercials.

JAN.			FEB.			MAR.		
	1	1		1	32		1	60
	2	2		2	33		2	61
	3	3		3	34		3	62
	4	4		4	35		4	63
	5	5		5	36		5	64
	6	6		6	37		6	65
	7	7		7	38		7	66
	8	8		8	39		8	67
	9	9		9	40		9	68
	10	10		10	41		10	69
	11	11		11	42		11	70
	12	12		12	43		12	71
	13	13		13	44		13	72
	14	14		14	45		14	73
	15	15		15	46		15	74
	16	16		16	47		16	75
	17	17		17	48		17	76
	18	18		18	49		18	77
	19	19		19	50		19	78
	20	20		20	51		20	79
	21	21		21	52		21	80
	22	22		22	53		22	81
	23	23		23	54		23	82
	24	24		24	55		24	83
	25	25		25	56		25	84
	26	26		26	57		26	85
	27	27		27	58		27	86
	28	28		28	59		28	87
	29	29						29	88
	30	30						30	89
	31	31						31	90

APR.	1	91	MAY	1	121	JUN	1	152
	2	92		2	122		2	153
	3	93		3	123		3	154
	4	94		4	124		4	155
	5	95		5	125		5	156
	6	96		6	126		6	157
	7	97		7	127		7	158
	8	98		8	128		8	159
	9	99		9	129		9	160
	10	100		10	130		10	161
	11	101		11	131		11	162
	12	102		12	132		12	163
	13	103		13	133		13	164
	14	104		14	134		14	165
	15	105		15	135		15	166
	16	106		16	136		16	167
	17	107		17	137		17	168
	18	108		18	138		18	169
	19	109		19	139		19	170
	20	110		20	140		20	171
	21	111		21	141		21	172
	22	112		22	142		22	173
	23	113		23	143		23	174
	24	114		24	144		24	175
	25	115		25	145		25	176
	26	116		26	146		26	177
	27	117		27	147		27	178
	28	118		28	148		28	179
	29	119		29	149		29	180
	30	120		30	150		30	181
				31	151			

JUL.	1	182	AUG.	1	213	SEPT.	1	244
	2	183		2	214		2	245
	3	184		3	215		3	246
	4	185		4	216		4	247
	5	186		5	217		5	248
	6	187		6	218		6	249
	7	188		7	219		7	250
	8	189		8	220		8	251
	9	190		9	221		9	252
	10	191		10	222		10	253
	11	192		11	223		11	254
	12	193		12	224		12	255
	13	194		13	225		13	256
	14	195		14	226		14	257
	15	196		15	227		15	258
	16	197		16	228		16	259
	17	198		17	229		17	260
	18	199		18	230		18	261
	19	200		19	231		19	262
	20	201		20	232		20	263
	21	202		21	233		21	264
	22	203		22	234		22	265
	23	204		23	235		23	266
	24	205		24	236		24	267
	25	206		25	237		25	268
	26	207		26	238		26	269
	27	208		27	239		27	270
	28	209		28	240		28	271
	29	210		29	241		29	272
	30	211		30	242		30	273
	31	212		31	243			

OCT.	1	274	NOV.	1	305	DEC.	1	335
	2	275		2	306		2	336
	3	276		3	307		3	337
	4	277		4	308		4	338
	5	278		5	309		5	339
	6	279		6	310		6	340
	7	280		7	311		7	341
	8	281		8	312		8	342
	9	282		9	313		9	343
	10	283		10	314		10	344
	11	284		11	315		11	345
	12	285		12	316		12	346
	13	286		13	317		13	347
	14	287		14	318		14	348
	15	288		15	319		15	349
	16	289		16	320		16	350
	17	290		17	321		17	351
	18	291		18	322		18	352
	19	292		19	323		19	353
	20	293		20	324		20	354
	21	294		21	325		21	355
	22	295		22	326		22	356
	23	296		23	327		23	357
	24	297		24	328		24	358
	25	298		25	329		25	359
	26	299		26	330		26	360
	27	300		27	331		27	361
	28	301		28	332		28	362
	29	302		29	333		29	363
	30	303		30	334		30	364
	31	304					31	365

Too simple, right? Right. Lifestyle, environment, habits, heredity, and a pile of other variables can and do affect how closely you will adhere to these norms. Perhaps the most critical added element in the equation is whether or not you are going to get hit by a truck. That would change everything. Stepping on a cobra would also be counter-productive.*

---

* Did you read about the guy who spent forty days in a room with twenty-four deadly snakes just to qualify for Guinness recognition? Can you imagine being the poor insurance guy who had him as a client? The nut's life expectancy was one forty-seventh of a second at any given moment. That's how long it takes a puff adder to wave you bye-bye. Serve him right if they spelled his name wrong.

The Ultimate Hink-Pink

Hink-Pink, Hinky-Pinky, Hinkity-Pinkity, Hinkitidy-Pinkitidy and extended variations ad infinitum are events in the field of unnecessary mental gymnastics at which you have repeatedly proved yourself capable of world class competition. Their common object is the condensation of obscure, the obscurer the better, hypothetical situations into continuous rhymes.

> Example: A New Yorker who teeters atop a piece of casual furniture and sprays movie film over a wine cabinet is a . . . KNICKERBOCKER WICKER-ROCKER LIQUOR-LOCKER FLICKER-FLOCKER.

I once thought that sentence was the state of the art, beyond which no one would ever progress. I thought that only until I heard from a poor deranged fellow named Jack Kearney. I don't know what institution holds Jack's commitment papers, but I hope it is long on security.

Anyone who could come up with the following is, I am sure you will agree, potentially dangerous.

A baseball pitcher with a scar on his cheek that made him look grumpy, who was well-known for eating well-done sixteen-ounce hamburgers, and had been wired by the networks so they could hear his conversations, on a plane flight from a small African nation where they had made him an honorary king and presented him with a magnificent ermine cape, crashed in the Atlantic the day before he was next scheduled to pitch, and was found dead is a . . . RENOWNED CROWNED GOWNED SOUND-WOUND FROWNED MOUND-BOUND DOWNED BROWNED-POUND-GROUND-ROUND HOUND FOUND DROWNED.

My sympathies, Jack.

The Continuing Adventures of Supercool, the Rubber Chicken

The procedure was described as routine, and the prognosis was excellent. "The odds are a million to one against anything going wrong," they assured me. "In by eight, out by four . . . absolutely nothing to worry about."

Bunk! Surgery is surgery, and if you happen to be the one, the million isn't worth the holes in a Swiss cheese sandwich. I was shaking in my Totes and said so.

"Aw, all you need is a little moral support," a caller soothed. "I know just the guy to help you get through it."

A clinically-trained stress therapist? Someone whose own septum had recently been successfully undeviated? Linda Ronstadt? None of the above. My courageous companion was to be one who had seen, done, and survived it all—Supercool, the rubber chicken. He or she (not having grown up on a farm, I have never been able to figure out which) arrived just in time to join me on the table. You had to be there to appreciate the look on that anesthesiologist's face. She could have turned into a prune danish for all I cared. I was there because I had to

be, but Supercool had volunteered. Now that's what I call a pal.

My fearless featherless friend has come a long way since that heroic introduction. Apparently assuming that any plucked samaritan willing to play security blanket for a basic piece of nose plumbing would be handy to have around in a real crunch, several of you other chickens have requested its company on crisis runs of your own. As a result, Supercool has helped sweat out more hair-raising adventures than Wonder Woman and Steve Austin combined. There have been eight nerve-wrenching flights to Europe and four to Hawaii, three major and innumerable minor operations, an appearance before a congressional investigations committee, speeches, sales meetings, job interviews, dental appointments, roller coaster rides, a driver's license exam, proposals, weddings, honeymoons, stints at Vegas gaming tables, and, well, you get the idea. That bird gets around.

A delightful tradition has grown with the log of fearsome missions accomplished. Each time old Supercluck (a pet name now) returns to the roost, a new airline ticket stub, hospital bill, or whatever is attached to the traveling coop. I wish I could remember and give credit to whoever came up with the idea, but like the inventor of the umbrella, his or her name is lost forever. Too bad. We are all afraid of things that go bump in the night, and that first proof of performance contributor gave us a way to help each other over the hump. Fear obviously isn't funny, but somehow a dark room doesn't seem quite so

Acknowledgement: Supercool's portraits are by Tony Romano. If you ever want a picture taken of your chicken, I recommend him.

ominous once you know that someone else has walked into and back out of it before you.

"Something" is understated. We are all afraid of some things. The average woman has 2.3 phobias, and men are even worse off with 3.2 of the little or not so little demons. Some fears, such as the fears of falling, of restraint, and of unexpected loud noises, are inherited at birth. The rest we pick up along the way. We could probably eliminate or at least control them by either addressing them head-on or recalling their original causes.

Coincidence?

Starting In The Middle was published in early 1979. In it, author Judith Wax wrote, "When the job required travel, I developed such a fear of airplanes my head trembled from takeoff to landing." Her comment appeared on page *191* of the book.

The May, 1979 issue of *Chicago* carried a review of the piece. An advertisement for American Airlines DC-10 flights to California was printed on the review page's reverse side and, when viewed against a light background, created a super-imposed double image of aircraft and author.

An advertisement for the book appeared in the same magazine's June issue. It faced page 191.

Judith Wax was a passenger aboard American Airlines' DC-10 Flight *#191* from Chicago to Los Angeles on May 25, 1979.

Acrophobia, the fear of height, is far and away our most common bogey, so big airlines and colleges run seminars on how to cope with it. Other widespread villains include: Agoraphobia, the fear of large, open space; Claustrophobia, fear of small, confined space; Ailurophobia, fear of cats; Anthrophobia, fear of human society; Algophobia, fear of pain; Astrophobia, fear of thunderstorms; Bacteriophobia, fear of disease; Chromatophobia, of money or wealth; Climacophobia, of falling down stairs; Demonophobia, of evil spirits; Dermatophobia, of touching skin; Doraphobia, of traffic; Erythrobia, of blushing; Elektrophobia, of electricity; Gephyrobophia, of crossing bridges; Heliophobia, of the sun; Hydrophobia, of water; Heresyphobia, of making decisions; Hylophobia, of woods or forests; Lyssophobia, dread of hydrophobia; Mysophobia, of dirt; Dysmorphobia, of being ugly; Neophobia, of novelty; Nyctophobia, of the dark; Ombrophobia, of rain; Pantophobia, of everything; Pharmacophobia, of medicine; Phasmophobia, of ghosts; Phobophobia, of one's own fears; Photophobia, of light; Pteronophobia, of being tickled by feathers; Sitiophobia, of food; and Zoophobia, the fear of animals. Hope you were paying attention. There will be a test later.

Sorry. I almost forgot one we encounter every day—tonguetiedophobia, the fear of talking on the radio. If I had a nickel for every on-air conversation begun with, "I'm so nervous," I'd be able to buy approximately nothing by the middle of next month. That is called "inflationphobia" and will be dealt with in excruciating detail at another place and time. There are hundreds, perhaps thousands, of phobias which someone has been brave and creative enough to name so far. Some of them seem laughable. That's healthy. It means your hang-ups are someone else's strong suits, and vice versa.

The message clearly stamped on every scrap of Supercool's nesting papers is, "We made it! You can too."

The heavy demand for a rubber chicken's services as placebo and surrogate worrier is understandable. Any turkey knows owls are wise, mules stubborn, foxes sly and chickens, well, chicken. A rubber giraffe or hippopotamus simply couldn't have pulled it off. I once thought of giving the job to a pig in hopes that it would improve its image. Those poor little fellas get a bad rap. They are really quite fastidious. They roll in the mud for precisely the same reason chic humans go to LaCosta. So why is it a fashionable beauty treatment for us and an expression of sloppiness for them? Why do woolly little lambs get such glowing press, when in truth they are the ones who really stink up the joint? Why indeed? Because lambs are lambs and pigs are pigs and chickens are chickens, that's why!

The French have a more enlightened idea about that. Some of their other ideas like BB and Catherine Deneuve (and Jean Claude Killy for the rest of you) have not been too wormy, so we ought to at least listen. They say the impressions that you have of animals tell a lot about you. Sort of a zoological ink-blot test. The key question, as I understand it, is "What animal would you like to be in your next life?" Your answer apparently blows your cover in this one, so be careful.

If, for the sake of improbable example, you think so much of monkeys that you want to be one the next time around, you are curious, alert, clever, sensitive, and bound to resemble the mope on the next page.

Chers Amis

Original French edition © 1976 Hier et Demain, Paris
Photographs © Frank Beyda
English-language edition © 1977 by Pomerica Press Limited
All rights reserved.

Hate the idea of being a monkey? That makes you broad-minded (I don't know which kind), generous of spirit, even-tempered, confident, and trustful.

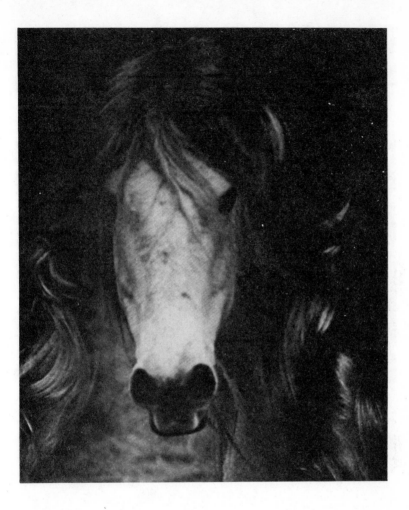

Do you want to be a Horse?

Next Time For Sure
You're a perfectionist with a lust for beauty, quality, and nobility. True love is your goal.

Neigh
You are a private, pragmatic, unemotional realist.

A Lion?

With Pride

You want to dominate
and conquer but have
an Achilles heel.
Watch your step.

Yuck!

You are sentimental,
modest, trustworthy,
a bit timid—a
person of taste.

A Dog?

Bark, Bark, Woof
You are totally
sensitive, intuitive,
sympathetic, adaptable,
and understanding.

Barf, Barf, Oof!
You are unsentimental,
energetic, strong-minded,
impatient—a real
individualist.

A Cat?

Purrfect
Fiercely individual,
aggressive, and charming,
you are extremely good
at handling crises.

A Litter Box Idea
You are moderately social
with a taste for order,
balance, and discretion.

156

A Peacock?

Aplume
You are more intellect than emotion. You are introspective and have trouble defining happiness.

Pluck It
You are ambitious, but your goal is not merely financial. You want, most of all, to be a valuable person.

A Butterfly?

Woo, Woo, Hubba
You are, as your photo
clearly shows, joyful,
whimsical, lucky, and
fascinating.

**Disgusting! Never heard
Such Filth!**
Not much of a blind date
are you?

Any more risqué shots like the last one and we'll probably get busted before we get to the good part. I'll rattle off the rest of your options sans the visual crutch. Before doing so, I want to credit the source. It's a marvelous fantasy piece, also French, named *Chers Amis* by Janet Belden Beyda (available from my publisher for $15.00). If you enjoyed these, you'll flip over her bears.

A Fish?

You're either a detached, disciplined person or a straightforward conservative, depending upon your orientation to the great beyond.

An Elephant?

Serene, even-tempered and loving, or youthful, spontaneous and undisciplined.

An Impala?

Either extremely goal-oriented or distrustful.

A Shellfish?

You would either prefer to live in an airtight compartment or let it all hang out.

A Donkey?

Very stable or flat-out adventurer. Nowhere in-between.

A Cockroach?

No data available. Essentially strange. Sounds good to me, though.

Animal associations have been honed to an even finer edge by our recently re-acquired good buddies, the Chinese. They peg your pet by the year you were born. (Those planets think of everything don't they.) To be accurate, some old Chinese Deities put the system together. Seems they once invited all of the world's animals to a big meeting and only twelve showed up. The Heavenly Folks were so appreciative, they gave each of the twelve a year-long commemoration party.

If you were born in:
    1900 — 31 January 1900 to 18 February 1901
    1912 — 18 February 1912 to 5 February 1913
    1924 — 5 February 1924 to 23 January 1925
    1936 — 24 January 1936 to 10 February 1937
    1948 — 10 February 1948 to 28 January 1949
    1960 — 28 January 1960 to 14 February 1961
you are a RAT!

Talk about pigs' PR problems, these first-cousins of rabbits and squirrels have already gotten enough bad advice image-wise to make Sherlock Holmes's Nemesis Moriarity, sound like a boy scout. Not so, apparently, on the far side of the wall. The Chinese actually revere the rat. They say people born under its sign are aggressive, gregarious, imaginative, honest, sentimental, generous, and make terrific clerks, pen-pushers, artists, businessmen, and politicians. Lady rats are said to be inveterate bargain hunters. Shakespeare, Tolstoy, Mozart, Marlon Brando, Lee Marvin (ask Michele), Irving Berlin, Jim Brown, Jennifer O'Neill, Kris Kristofferson, and Artis Gilmore are all rats of note.

A birthdate in the following years:
    1901 — 19 February 1901 to 7 February 1902
    1913 — 6 February 1913 to 25 January 1914
    1925 — 24 January 1925 to 12 February 1926
    1937 — 11 February 1937 to 30 January 1938
    1949 — 29 January 1949 to 16 February 1950
    1961 — 15 February 1961 to 4 February 1962
makes you a Buffalo.

Buffalo are patient, quiet, reserved, slow, retiring, stable, precise, methodical, original, intelligent, boorish, contemplative, fanatical, chauvinistic, bigoted, temperamental, violent, dangerous, stubborn, tranquil, and obstinate. (They certainly sound swell, don't they?) Lady

Buffalo include: Napoleon, Hitler, Walt Disney, Paul Newman, Robert Redford, Johnny Carson, MTM, Gerald Ford, Jesse Owens, Jane Fonda, Michael Landon, Charlie Chaplin, and all us recent genius types listed earlier. Apparently the Chinese do not care at all for talk shows or old movies.

A birthdate in the years:

    1902 — 8 February 1902 to 28 January 1903
    1914 — 26 January 1914 to 13 February 1915
    1926 — 3 February 1926 to 1 February 1927
    1938 — 31 January 1938 to 18 February 1939
    1950 — 17 February 1950 to 5 February 1951
    1962 — 5 February 1962 to 24 January 1963

makes you a Tiger.

Tigers are critical, undisciplined, hot-tempered, reckless, revolutionary, disobedient, demanding, passionate, sensitive, emotional, capable of profound thought. They are risk-taking leaders who are rarely happy in love. Exceptional Tigers are Joe Louis, Ray Kroc, Joe D'Maggio, Marilyn Monroe, Natalie Wood, Mohammed, Ho Chi Minh, Bill Cosby, and Karl Marx.

    1903 — 29 January 1903 to 15 February 1904
    1915 — 14 February 1915 to 2 February 1916
    1927 — 2 February 1927 to 22 January 1928
    1939 — 19 February 1939 to 7 February 1940
    1951 — 6 February 1951 to 26 January 1952
    1963 — 25 January 1963 to 12 February 1964

These years of entry make you a Cat. Cats are gifted, ambitious, agreeable, discreet, refined, virtuous, sophisticated, cultured, charming, pedantic, conservative, timid, clever, affectionate, helpful, but lack a strong sense of family. The she-cat could shine in any field that demands taste and good presentation. Some famous cats are Confucius, Luther, Marie Antoinette, Red Grange,

Bob Hope, Frank Sinatra, Judy Collins, Orson Welles, Lawrence Welk, John Dillinger, Saul Bellow, Harry Belafonte, Einstein, Fidel Castro, Peter Falk, and Stalin.

1904 — 16 February 1904 to 3 February 1905
1916 — 3 February 1916 to 22 January 1917
1928 — 23 January 1928 to 9 February 1929
1940 — 8 February 1940 to 26 January 1941
1952 — 27 January 1952 to 13 February 1953
1964 — 13 February 1964 to 1 February 1965

are dates of the Dragon.

Dragons are healthy, vital, energetic, straightforward, gullible, naive, scrupulous, irritable, stubborn, impetuous, enthusiastic, proud, tenacious, lucky, and willful. In other words a Dragon is a loud-mouthed conquering warrior. The female of the species will always be surrounded by men. Cary Grant, Walter Chronkite, James Garner, Salvador Dali, Dionne Warwick, Freud, Joan of Arc, and Ringo Starr head the list.

1905 — 4 February 1905 to 24 January 1906
1917 — 23 January 1917 to 10 February 1918
1929 — 10 February 1929 to 30 January 1930
1941 — 27 January 1941 to 14 February 1942
1953 — 14 February 1953 to 2 February 1954
1965 — 2 February 1965 to 20 January 1966

The Serpent. Unlike those of us in the west who recoil, Asians venerate the serpent for its intelligence and wisdom. Serpents are sentimental, humorous, talkative, intellectual, philosophical, intuitive, possessive, and jealous. Notables include Darwin, Copernicus, Warren Beatty, Ingrid Bergman, Bob Newhart, Gandhi, Mao Tse-tung, Paul Anka, Edgar Allen Poe, Bob Dylan, Jacqueline Kennedy Onassis, Ryan O'Neal, and Picasso.

1906 — 25 January 1906 to 12 February 1907
1918 — 11 February 1918 to 31 January 1919

1930 — 31 January 1930 to 16 February 1931
1942 — 15 February 1942 to 4 February 1943
1954 — 3 February 1954 to 23 January 1955
1966 — 21 January 1966 to 8 February 1967

The Horse. Horses are gay (old sense), likable, popular, gifted, ambitious, impatient, remorseless, egocentric, and weak in relations with the opposite sex—a potentially successful politician or entertainer. Ella Fitzgerald, Paul McCartney, Muhammad Ali, Barbra Streisand, Rembrandt, FDR, Khrushchev, Clint Eastwood, and Dick Butkus, to name a few.

1907 — 13 February 1907 to 1 February 1908
1919 — 1 February 1919 to 19 February 1920
1931 — 17 February 1931 to 5 February 1932
1943 — 5 February 1943 to 24 January 1944
1955 — 24 January 1955 to 11 February 1956
1967 — 9 February 1967 to 29 January 1968

You are a Goat. The Goat is elegant, artistic, affectionate, hesitant, pessimistic, discontent, exasperating, capricious, feminine, sweet, dishonest, religious, dependent, obedient—definitely not the leadership model. Successful goats are or have been George Halas, Joni Mitchell, Valentino, Laurence Olivier, Michelangelo, John Wayne, Alan Alda, Chuck Percy, and Leslie Uggams.

1908 — 2 February 1908 to 21 January 1909
1920 — 20 February 1920 to 8 February 1921
1932 — 6 February 1932 to 25 January 1933
1944 — 25 January 1944 to 12 February 1945
1956 — 12 February 1956 to 30 January 1957
1968 — 30 January 1968 to 16 February 1969

The Monkey. Monkeys are about what you'd expect them to be. Crafty, sociable, malicious, playful, friendly, inventive, vain, unstable, naughty, affectionate, critical. Their mixed barrel includes Ray Charles, Diana Ross,

THE WALLY PHILLIPS PEOPLE BOOK

Bette Davis, Liberace, da Vinci, LBJ, Truman, Johnny
Cash, Angie Dickinson, and Julius Caesar.
    1909 — 22 January 1909 to 9 February 1910
    1921 — 9 February 1921 to 27 January 1922
    1933 — 26 January 1933 to 13 February 1934
    1945 — 13 February 1945 to 1 February 1946
    1957 — 31 January 1957 to 17 February 1958
    1969 — 17 February 1969 to 5 February 1970
    The Chicken. The Chicken is frank, eccentric, flamboyant in dress, agrarian, conservative, bragging, brilliant, extravagant, yet unfulfilled. Some famous Chickens—Wagner, Liza Minelli, Neil Diamond, Steve Allen, Mia Farrow, Flip Wilson, Bill Mauldin, Katherine Hepburn and, of course, my main man or whatever—Supercool.
    1910 — 10 February 1910 to 29 January 1911
    1922 — 28 January 1922 to 15 February 1923
    1934 — 14 February 1934 to 3 February 1935
    1946 — 2 February 1946 to 21 January 1947
    1958 — 18 February 1958 to 7 February 1959
    The Dog. Dogs are restless, alert, guarded, cynical, antisocial, banal, sincere, moral, generous, parochial—ideally suited for work as labor leaders, priests, or teachers. Famous Dogs—Ralph Nader, Barbara Eden, Diahann Carole, Lenin, Voltaire, Socrates, Candice Bergen, Carol Burnett, and the Dione quints.
    1911 — 30 January 1911 to 17 February 1912
    1923 — 16 February 1923 to 4 February 1924
    1935 — 4 February 1935 to 23 January 1936
    1947 — 22 January 1947 to 9 February 1948
    1959 — 8 February 1959 to 27 January 1960
    The Pig. All right, let's hear it for the good guys! Yeah! Right on, Porky. If the Chinese are so fond of rats and snakes, they must love the pig. Yep, they say swine are

gallant, helpful, pure, sincere, intelligent, joyful, rowdy, authoritative, private, attentive, conscientious, and definitely not sloppy. The first Rockefeller, the first Rothschild, the first Ford, Saint Ignatius Loyola, Dr. Schweitzer, Burt Reynolds, Perry Como, Archie Bunker, Lucille Ball, Elvis, Henry VIII, Woody Allen, and O. J. Simpson—all Pigs.

Much more detailed versions of all these important matters are buried in piles in my office somewhere. If you want to know the entire scoop, give me a call and I'll send them to you. In the meantime, be kind to any animal secure enough to, unlike humans, admit it is an animal. It may be the key to something important.

The Language
Lesson #3

Stay Current

If you want the words you use to say what you mean, use words that still mean what you want to say. Words like gay, pig, joint, heavy, and get down are representative potential trouble spots for those of you who have chosen to grow up in sync with your bodies. Be careful how you choose them.

This isn't a new problem, of course. I can remember hearing Lenny Bruce build an entire routine around the problem way back before I was doing Bill Murray impersonations. Between puffs, squints, tiffs with the law, and whatever else he could think of to harm himself, Lenny would peek out at the world the rest of us lived in and notice it. He once noticed that ladies of the evening weren't being called prostitutes anymore. Quality writers turned commercial hacks were, however, said to be prostituting their talents. If, he therefore further noted, one of the former happened to pay a business call on one of the latter, it would be a hooker knocking on the door and a prostitute answering.

It is interesting to note that even Lenny has undergone

something of an image face-lift over the years. Maybe if he hadn't been quite as current (as in events) then, he'd still be current (as in alive) now.

P.S. I know one word you'll never have to worry about. It's the only English word that is used and means the same thing everywhere in the world. Tell you about it on page 170.

The Boot Hill of Dated Fad Phrases

bar

In Search
Of The Elusive
Vanishing Googol

The consensus is that either rats or insects will eventually inherit the earth. Science fiction buffs, documentary movie makers, and other people who wear berets have determined that, because they multiply and adapt so quickly, these animals will survive the longest. Their squeamy predictions may come true in the long, long run, but I perceive a more imminent threat to our well-being. I refer, of course, to the ever-growing menace of numbers.

Pick a field, any field. Now slip it back into the deck and try to imagine it in numberless terms. Sports without scores? Business without a bottom line? TV without ratings? Dieting without a scale? It can't be done. No matter where you turn, decimals and ciphers abound. They regulate habits, judge performance, predict bodily function, identify, codify, and glut the information storage tanks of our collective brain. Their ambition is insatiable. For random evidence, consider the postal system. A street address in Chicago, Illinois was once enough to get your bills, jury duty notices, chain letters, and occupant flyers delivered. Then came zip codes. I have heard that those cumbersome five-digit versions which have

THE WALLY PHILLIPS PEOPLE BOOK

taken us a decade to not quite memorize are about to spin off a new generation nine numbers long. Once that mission is accomplished, their emphasis will undoubtedly turn again to ever more confusing telephone numbers, social security numbers, delicatessen waiting line numbers, and on and on and on.

Worse, when such brute force tactics occasionally fail, numbers are entirely capable of turning on the charm and further undermining our defenses by intriguing us with seemingly innocent statistical oddities and games. A classic guerilla strategy.

Exhibit A:

When, toward the end of a conversation during which he has told us, "If the sun was a cherry pit and the earth a grain of sand three feet away, the nearest star would be another cherry pit 140 miles away," the man from the Adler Planetarium adds, "Although only nine or ten thousand stars are visible to the naked eye, there are billions of them in our galaxy alone, and billions of galaxies in the universe," we are blown away. Not as blown away as we were by trying to make sense of that sentence perhaps, but definitely impressed. Our minds simply can't handle a concept as abstract as billions of anything. Once you pass a million, everything tends to become so much corned beef hash. I mean, who knows what a billion looks or feels or tastes like?

Recognizing an opportunity, numbers collaborators smiled reassuringly and offered to put it in terms we could grasp. "One million seconds lasts twelve days," one helpful numerologist politely explained. "One billion seconds lasts 32 YEARS!"

"Eureka! I've got it!" I screamed. (Actually, I have

never screamed or even mumbled eureka in my entire life, except during a few vacuum cleaner commercials, but it seems like a nice enthusiastic word, so I decided to give it a break.)

"No, not really," my mentor cautioned. "That would only be true if you were working with American or French seconds. In England and Germany the comparison would have been 32,000 years for a billion seconds."

As I have by now noted ad nauseam, hard-hats catch what Mensa types miss, and the reverse is also true, so together we know everything. As I may have also mentioned, it doesn't take a whole lot to get a relatively heated discussion started on any topic. The debate was on, and I was soon to learn that, contrary to the opinion of the first caller, seconds do in fact tick and tock the same regardless of their geography, but like temperature, the size of Pepsi bottles, and almost everything else, we measure them differently. This is as it should be.

𝔓𝔥𝔦𝔩𝔩𝔦𝔭𝔰'𝔰 𝔒𝔱𝔥𝔢𝔯 𝔏𝔞𝔴: About some things people debate. About others they argue. Sex, Religion, Politics, Abortion, Capital Punishment, Gun Control, the ERA, and Metric Conversion all belong in column B. The remainder of that morning's program was not filled with what you would call bland interaction.

Right or wrong, here were its factual conclusions. An official American billion (like its Gallic counterpart) is made up of one thousand millions, whereas a British billion (also a German) is one million millions. A high-roller here is a virtual piker there, which probably comes as close to explaining ex-patriate Beatle John Lennon as anything in the language ever will. After all, it is a lot easier to be a rich spiritual guru of leftover counter-culture drop-outs than a poor one.

A Fun Game For
Rich Counter-Culturists
And Their Gurus

Place your hand or Swiss bank account book over all but the very top number in the column below. Now, sliding the shield down to reveal only one number at a time, add them aloud.

$$1,000$$
$$40$$
$$1,000$$
$$30$$
$$1,000$$
$$20$$
$$1,000$$
$$10$$

What did you come up with? 5,000? Great. Now add them with a pencil _____.

Quick, pick one of the following numbers.

1   2   3   4   5

Psychiatrists suggest (psychiatrists never flat-out say anything; suggesting, to them, is pretty strong stuff) that most of us pick the number three because of our subliminal reverence for the mother/father/child unit of family. Many Christian clerics credit the Trinity. Advertising agency creative directors point to that number's inherently interesting bubbles and prongs (the billboard on page 101 seems to favor the latter). Whatever. Three comes up approximately ninety-five percent of the time.

Which, for no conscious reason, brings to mind everyone's all-time favorite numbers gambit. It is at least sixty years old and brand new to every generation that comes along.

Three dudes checked into a hotel. The part-time desk clerk on duty didn't remember how much to charge for a room but thought $30 sounded about right. Each cat gave him a ten dollar bill. (Bonus surprise game within a game: What kind of car appears on the backside of ten dollar bills?) When the hotel's manager learned of the transaction, he said the room rent should have been only $25, which proves how old this thing really is, and dispatched the clerk to return the difference. On his way to the room, the clerk realized that the three guests would have difficulty dividing five dollars evenly, so he decided to be a nice guy and only give them three instead.

What we have here is a confusing situation. Each of the three guys had now paid $9. That makes $27 total. The clerk kept $2. That equals $29, right? What happened to the other dollar?

Fascinating stuff, huh? Insidious is more like it. By the time you realize what is happening, it is too late. Numbers have nibbled away yet another chunk of armor.

What good does playing answerless games and knowing the difference between a million, a billion, our national debt of half a trillion,* or any other illion do Mr. and Mrs. Youanme anyway? Most of us have enough problems just trying to stretch the budget around an occasional Big Mac attack, for databank's sake.

---

*Uncle Sam is now spending more than $15,000 a second. A second! That half a trillion figure is five hundred times as mind-boggling than the billion stuff. It is enough to buy 172,951,000 new automobiles, give every person in the world $120, or make every man, woman, and child in Atlanta a millionaire. Oh well, it's only money, and nowhere near as intimidating as a googol. That's the ultimate number—any digit plus one hundred zeroes. A British mathematician's six-year-old named it. True story.

Sound flip? Inflation is anything but. The numbers tell the story. Between 1972 and 1979, the price of those two all beef patties, special sauce, lettuce, cheese, pickles, and onions on a sesame seed bun rose 73%. Of course you didn't get one of those cute styrofoam boxes with the sandwich back in '72, and the increase is really rather moderate by comparison to Dixie Cup refills, gas heat, Mercedes-Benz, palm trees, asparagus, ocean perch, Stewart's Private Blend Coffee, and Bazooka sugarless gum. They spiraled anywhere from 163% to 300% during the same period. Even they seem almost reasonable next to alfalfa seeds which went up a breathtaking 574% a pound.

I know this is going to require tremendous sacrifice, but frankly, I think you ought to forget about your secret family alfalfa seed recipes for a while. Tell the kids they'll have to settle for filet and caviar until the market levels off.

On the brighter side, the price of at least one necessity has actually been declining steadily over the years. An average radio costs less today than it did thirty years ago. For some reason, I've never been able to get as excited about that phenomenon as I know I should. Sheer weight of contrary trends, I suppose. I read recently that, at the rate we're going, a car is going to cost about $200,000 by the middle of the next century, and that is if you can get gasohol to make it run. Numismatists like Leonard Stark's great-grandchildren will probably be doing fast business with coin collectors in search of antique hundred-dollar bus tokens.

You know it and I know it. There is only one way we are ever going to be able to amass enough of a fortune to survive.

Flip A Coin

"Yep. That's all there is to it," our guest expert insisted. "The one and only guaranteed, fail-safe, sure-fire way to fend off the slings and arrows of outrageous fortune (boy, that Jimmy the Greek can sure be a golden-tongued devil when he wants to be) is to get yourself a coin, walk right into the nearest watering hole, and offer to let anyone in the joint call it for a buck." He bet me two bits I could retire within a year if I followed the instructions. "The odds are fifty-fifty for either side on every toss," he chuckled knowingly, "but seven out of ten people call 'heads' when given the option. . . a license to print money if I have ever heard one."

"So, why aren't there a bunch of billionaires wandering in and out of bars all over town?" I asked. After a few expert-sounding harumpfs, the wiz allowed as how, well, yes, there was one tiny trick involved. "You have to start out with a smart coin—one with a good memory," he said. "Most coins are not very bright; they are so dull, in fact, that they can't even remember which way they landed the last time around and have to start counting all over again on every flip." And you wonder why Cynthia Socialite and her cronies complain about how difficult it is to get good help these days? I mean, when you can't even count on the consistency of United States currency, what's left? Think Japanese yen are any good for flipping? How about transistors?

Let's call Jimmy some day next week and find out. On him we can rely. If he doesn't know an answer, he's always able and willing to make one up.

In the meantime, maybe you should hedge against inflation by winning the lottery instead. It is quicker than flipping coins, almost as lucrative, and the odds are a nice, predictable, 30-million-to-one on every throw. Oh, come on. You aren't going to let a little thing like that intimidate you. Where is your spirit of adventure? What would Wilbur and Orville Oddsbucker have thought? Heck, it could be a lot worse. You could be hoping for quintuplets and facing a 40,960,000-to-1 shot, or trying to be the one person in 2,235,197,406,895,366,301,-559,999 to deal four perfect bridge hands. Why, with a solid chance in every 197 to double your ante, the lottery is a relative piece of cake.*

Not enough skill involved, you say? Prefer some cerebral challenge with your action? No problem. Try poker, craps, roulette, golf, tennis, bingo, naming the seven dwarfs,† or just plain living. They're all a gamble.

---

* For a compendium of sports cliches, including "a can of corn" and the increasingly popular "they've got old Mo Mentum on their side," please tune in any broadcast of anything featuring Howard Cosell.

† For details, stay up and watch the Robert Altman film with a plot next time it is on the tube.

Your odds are:

1,350,000 to 1 against being hit by lightning.
649,000 to 1 against being dealt a royal flush.
512,000 to 1 against having quadruplets.
72,193 to 1 against being dealt a straight flush.
54,133 to 1 against being dealt four aces.
35,308 to 1 against getting bingo within five calls.
8,600 to 1 against getting a hole in one on a par three hole (assuming that you normally hit the green on two out of five tee shots, which further assumes that you do not play the game anything like I do).
1,827 to 1 against being dealt a Yarborough—thirteen cards with none higher than a nine.
38 to 1 against picking a correct roulette number and being paid 35 to 1 for your trouble.
12 to 1 against either being left-handed or filling an inside straight.
4.5 to 1 against rolling a natural (seven or eleven) in craps.

Remember, I prefaced that list by saying those were *your* odds. They obviously don't apply to everyone. Lee Trevino, for example, is much more likely to get a hole in one or be struck by lightning than the average player. Here he is describing the feeling generated by either experience to a well-known Chicago area golf phenomenon named Señor Phillips.

The fun-loving Mr. Trevino later explained that he had been able to realistically re-create the precise sensation with the help of fellow golf pro Don Wegrzyn, who had secretly filled Mr. Phillips's canteen with imported water of unknown origin.

Nor do the normal probabilities affect the winning ratios of such sportsmen as Minnesota Fats, Bobby Riggs, or poker king Arizona Slim. With hustle and determination, each has risen to the front rank of his respective profession. This is, by the way, rumored to be of great interest to certain IRS minions who have long marveled at their ability to get by on so little.* No such confusion regarding Muhammad Ali. As at almost everything else, he is a champion's champion at paying taxes. The very idea of laying odds, any odds, against his performance is laughable. The champ is so good at winning, he wins doing things he doesn't even know how to do. Before donning the silks for a recent charity harness race at Maywood Park, for example, he confidently declared that he and his less than enthusiastic horse (tugging 240+ pounds of champion around a race track in the middle of February isn't exactly kicks, you know) would not only win the trot, but would set a new world record in the process. They did! The minor facts that no race had ever before been run at that particular distance, thus assuring a record, and that the other drivers had to all but break their horses' necks to stay behind are trifling details. Like Lady Godiva, who put everything she had on a horse, Ali risks it all on every roll. He puts his money where his mouth is. He wins.

Losers still outnumber winners, but as a result of our society's terribly imbalanced value system, they go virtually unnoticed and unappreciated. While superstars get candy bars named in their honor, losers get only derisive jeers. Enough! I hereby proclaim and establish

---

* Please don't take this line too seriously. "Rumored" is roughly synonymous with "made-up." Remember the hot rumor about the hammer and sickle being printed on the Kennedy half-dollars? They turned out to be the engraver's initials.

the Loser's Hall of Fame. My initial group of nominees
are:
- The anonymous fat man who once fell asleep at a
  luau with an apple in his mouth.
- Jim Marshall, the Minnesota Vikings' venerable de-
  fensive end, who picked up a fumble and trium-
  phantly raced eighty yards in the wrong direction.
- The poor sap who tried to hold up a MacDonald's in
  Milwaukee with a banana and was so nervous that
  he forgot to put it in his pocket.
- Everyone who gave Notre Dame and points in the
  1978 Cotton Bowl game against Texas, and everyone
  who gave Houston and points in '79.

"And the winner is . . . may I have the envelope,
please . . . oh, wow! A write-in candidate, Arthur Allaway!"

Although high-rolling Art is legendary in betting circles, I realize that a few of you clean livers (you know, the
six of you really ought to get together and start a club so
you would have something to do) may not be familiar
with his award-winning escapades. Mr. Allaway was
once, yes this is unfortunately a posthumous presentation, the single most inveterate and successful bettor in
the world. He would bet on anything, and I do mean
anything.

"How do you feel?" you might casually ask.

"What's the spread?" he would reply.

Well one day, *the* day in fact, Art and his best friend
Ralph Railbird were on the last leg of a Love Boat cruise
which one or the other of them had won at a church
bazaar. As the photogenic floating playpen is equipped
with every amenity short of a casino and race track, most
folks think it is the greatest thing since back rubs. Not Art

and Ralph. Three days of inaction had driven them both right up the bulkheads. Finally, they couldn't take it any longer. Having noted their delayed arrival at every intermediate port, and knowing that the ship couldn't possibly reach its ultimate destination anywhere close to the intinerary's ETA, Art nudged Ralph and said, "Ten million bucks say we don't pull in until seven P.M." Having overheard the ship's captain arranging a six o'clock date with the cabaret singer only that morning, Ralph smirked, "You're covered."

The hours passed slowly, and Art suddenly realized that the damn boat was going one hell of a lot faster than it had been. Land was in sight at 4:58 P.M. Chagrin and dismay! This had the makings of a major setback to both his wallet and his reputation. Friends, you don't get to be the single most inveterate and successful gambler in the world on luck alone. Spying a young couple holding hands at the rail, he saw and seized his opportunity. He raced screaming toward them, and passing just inches to their left, hurtled himself madly over the side.

On the way to his watery salvation from ruin and dishonor, Art let out one last delicious salute to his genius. He knew, you see, that his swim would be short-lived. The couple would be momentarily dazed by the horror, then instantly alert the crew to the terror of a man overboard. The ship would have to stop, lower a dinghy, rescue him, and in the process, lose more than enough time to give old Ralph a case of permanent dyspepsia.

Unfortunately for Art, however, not Ralph, the young man and woman at the rail were not only in love, they were both deaf and blind as well. Both would always remember the incredible serenity of their last honeymooning day at sea. It had been absolutely perfect, except for that one fleeting chill breeze moments before they had docked.

The average human does not float long enough in salt water to catch a once-a-week Love Boat. Arthur Allaway was last seen giving Jaws 3 to 1 on heartburn if he didn't back off.

What about Ralph? A bitter man, I fear. He had to pay for that as yet incomplete contract on his one-time pal who had squelched on their biggest bet ever, and his broker had recommended Miami Beach casino sites over alfalfa seeds. Now the only things this desolate soul has left to keep him going are the weekly parlay cards during football season. Him and a few million other coin-headed schnooks.

Sure, betting on football games is as American as chocolate cream pie. Yes, I know "everyone does it." My only question is, "Who needs the card?"

"They make it official . . . give all the right point spreads and everything."

"The odds. You can get back 6, 46, even 101 to 1 with a winner."

"Oh, so what. Who does it hurt?"

The litany of parlay card players' retorts is as long and predictable as it is misguided. For openers (Notice the authentic gambling jargon throughout this part? Man, this is a class production.), those important "official point spreads" are about as tough to find as mosquitoes in August. Next time you're having trouble finding them, check any newspaper, sportscast, or six-year-old kid on the block. Failing, go ahead and get a card. As though you didn't know, they look a lot like this. As a matter of fact, since this is one, they look exactly like this.

SAT. and SUN. SEPT. 26th and 27th

1 Cornell	—1	2 Colgate	—1
3 Auburn	—1	4 Tennessee	—1
5 T.C.U.	—1	6 Wisconsin	—1
7 California		8 Indiana	+3
9 Pittsburgh		10 Baylor	+3
11 Tulane		12 Illinois	+3
(13) Penn St.		14 Colorado	+6
15 Alabama		16 Florida	+6
17 Georgia Tech.		18 Miami Fla.	+7
19 Michigan		20 Washington	+7
21 Michigan St.		22 Wash. St.	+10
23 Missouri		24 Air Force	+10
25 Oklahoma		26 Oregon St.	+13
(27) Notre Dame		28 Purdue	+13
29 U.C.L.A.		30 Northwestern	+13
31 Texas		32 Texas Tech.	+20

SUNDAY

33 Pittsburgh	—1	34 Denver	—1
35 San Francisco	—1	36 Cleveland	—1
37 St. Louis		38 Washington	+3
(39) Oakland		40 San Diego	+3
41 Green Bay		42 Atlanta	+6
43 Houston		44 Miami	+7
45 Bears		46 Philadelphia	+10
47 Dallas		48 N. Y. Giants	+10
49 N. Y. Jets		50 Boston	+13
51 Detroit		52 Cincinnati	+14
53 Minnesota		54 New Orleans	+19
(55) L. A. Rams		56 Buffalo	+19

3 — 6
4 — 11
5 — 16
6 — 31
7 — 46
8 — 61
9 — 76
10 — 101
9 of 10 — 16

TIES ELIMINATE SELECTIONS
NOT TO BE SOLD

VOID OUTSIDE OF ILLINOIS

N° 25605

As the flip side, shown here on the left, clearly shows, the card's "good odds" offer bettors a chance to lose all ties and get back a fraction of what the real odds against their getting *anything* back are. Am I going too fast for you? This is straight scoop. The card's top pay-out is 101 to 1 for picking ten games on the money. The odds against hitting it, no matter how well you remember the game from when you were an all-conference honorable mention back in high school, are 12,472 to 1. If that's good, I cringe to imagine your definition of bad.

Oh yeah, I almost forgot about the "who does it hurt?" part. Everyone. It hurts me. It hurts you. It hurts everybody else except maybe the civic-minded folks who put it out. According to police officers who get a chance to see some of the people it hurts up real close, all that harmless little parlay card bet of yours does is buy about two bucks worth of murder, prostitution, drug traffic, corruption, and filth. Other than that, I guess it's okay.

If you enjoy betting on the Cowboys or Steelers or even the Bears, and we apparently all do at one time or another, by all means do so. But do it with a neighbor or the car pool or your wife, not the boys. You can still become independently wealthy, and who knows, you might eventually get to take a nice boat ride somewhere.

The Equal Rights Amendment

Forget what you've heard about it. This is what it says:

> EQUALITY OF RIGHTS UNDER THE LAW SHALL
> NOT BE DENIED OR ABRIDGED BY THE UNITED
> STATES OR BY ANY STATE ON ACCOUNT OF SEX.
> CONGRESS AND SEVERAL STATES SHALL HAVE
> POWER WITHIN THEIR RESPECTIVE JURISDIC-
> TIONS TO ENFORCE THIS ARTICLE BY APPROPRI-
> ATE LEGISLATION.

Pretty inflammatory material, all right. No wonder
Phyllis and her friends are so excited. Why, if something
as controversial as that were enacted, women might be
forced to go to baseball games, chew tobacco, and who
knows what all.

The Mavin
Has Spoken

The *Sun-Times* Kup's column has been a day-in day-out barometer of the Chicago scene for more than three decades. Like its creator's nationally syndicated television conversations, it is a cosmopolitan marvel of crisp, lucid reportage. As such, however, it is bound by the restraints of journalistic composition and objectivity. Seldom has the resultant coverage of everything from internecine political warfare to pretty-people minutiae allowed Irv Kupcinet's more reflective side, his insight and sensitivity, to show through. It is, therefore, with pride and genuine humility, that the next several pages offer for the first time in print and as a monument to the man's contributions, a comprehensive digest of invaluable lessons concerning life, living, and loving which Kup has taken the time to teach me, in spite of his incredibly hectic schedule.

THE MAVIN HAS SPOKEN

Inspiring, ain't it?

Speaking of monuments, I have one that nobody can touch. Not Ulysses S. Grant, not King Tut, not even hamburger king Ray Kroc with his arch over the Mississippi. Mine stands about a thousand feet above the rest and took death-defying effort to create. Unfortunately, you can't see it because of the slab of marble someone stuck on top of it, but it's there. Here's proof.

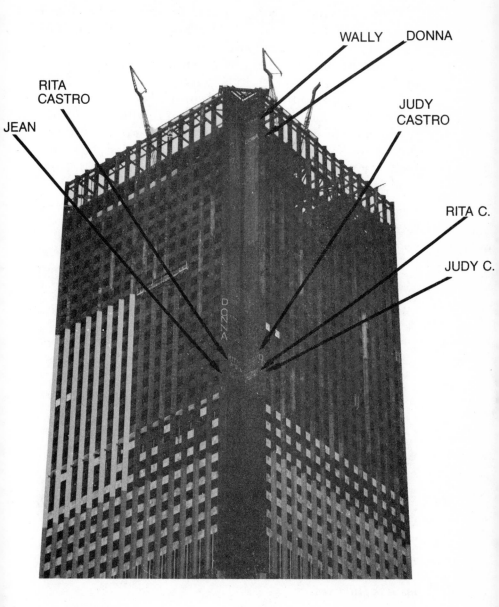

That was what the Standard Oil Building looked like a few weeks before it officially began adding its touch of class to Chicago's already magnificent skyline. A listener in a nearby office called one morning and delivered an understandably incredulous play-by-play of someone named Donna's number one admirer's breath-taking attempt to immortalize her. The urban mountain climber in question apparently had his radio on and enjoyed the notoriety. As an expression of his appreciation, he scribbled my name up there too. Even gave me top billing. Hope that didn't turn off Donna.

This isn't the guy who did the artwork, but when it comes to impossible dream stuff, he's my kind of hero. As the credit card commercial says, his face may not be familiar, but his achievement is Hillaryesque.

The Titanic's Last Lifeboat ... That Sinking Feeling

Super-achievers in any field are supposedly motivated by one of three primary drives—love, power, or the lust for achievement itself. My hunches about the random movers and shakers listed below are checked on the left. How do they match up with yours?

Love	Power	Achievement		Love	Power	Achievement
	√		Jimmy Carter			
		√	Gloria Steinem			
		√	Hugh Hefner			
	√		Barbra Streisand			
		√	Ralph Nader			
√			Rev. Martin Luther King			
		√	Chagall			
√		√	Helen Keller			
√			Schweitzer			
	√		Phyllis Schlafly			

195

Love	Power	Achievement		Love	Power	Achievem...
✓			Gandhi			
	✓		Kissinger			
		✓	Chris Columbus			
		✓	Bob Hope			
		✓	Abraham Lincoln			
	✓		Bonnie Parker			
		✓	Karl Marx			
$	$	$	Xaviera Hollander			
		✓	Gwendolyn Brooks			
	✓		Adolph Hitler			

Hey, no fair checking everything and saying they were all into the love of achievement and power.

Regardless of their true motives, these famous and/or infamous luminaries have all had something in common—impact. They have all mattered to our world, and for better or worse, they have all had an effect upon our lives. According to *The 100* by Michael Hart, there are quite a few of them we'd have had a tough time getting along without. He is probably right about that, but I'm not sure I would agree with the group he might rank as essential. Abe Lincoln didn't even make it into his book. As if that weren't bad enough, neither did Jack Brickhouse.

It's the same old story again and again. Values are an individual thing. I am forever fascinated when our conversations turn to the relative worth of various people. No one, let me re-phrase that—NO ONE, gets unanimous acclaim. A couple of running "what if" games underscore the point.

The Dinner Party

The game's premise is simple. You are having a very special dinner party to which you may invite any six people who have ever lived. The only *personae non gratae* (unwelcome guests, for those of you who have never watched William F. Buckley and Gore Vidal do anything together or alone) are family and friends. You can see them anytime. Now, whom would you invite?

Four interesting things usually happen when people answer that question. First, of course, we tell a good deal about ourselves by the guest list we assemble. Second, we tend to invite darned near the same type of person from different eras—all militarists, artists, con men, or similarly similar people. Third, a guest thought to be extremely evil—Hitler for the sake of repugnant argument—is invariably immediately followed by Jesus Christ or some equivalent. The reverse pattern also applies. Fourth, and perhaps most significant, with the exception of an occasional male respondent's leering overture in the direction of some sex bomb, we ignore women almost entirely. With but a place or two left at the table, this chauvinistic oversight is normally caught, and the party-giver belches Barbara Walters or Margaret Mead in unthinking panic.

There is no particular punch line to any of this. It is what I'm sure is known in some trade somewhere as an entertaining diversion. Try it sometime. If your parties are anything like the ones I usually attend, they could use a lift.

Titanic's Last Lifeboat

Another exercise with the same basic ingredients is the game of "Titanic's Last Lifeboat." Since its consequences are somewhat more dramatic for the participants, its mirror of our subjective values is proportionally clearer.

This time you aren't a host or hostess. You are the only qualified sailor aboard the last functioning lifeboat from a sunken ship at sea. Without you, no one can survive, not even your scruffy pal who has valiantly dog-paddled to your side and is, even at this moment, staring confidently in your direction. Unfortunately, however, your craft is beginning to swamp because of its overload. You must throw someone overboard to keep it and you and everyone else from going under.

At this juncture, you are supposed to decide whom to toss from a list of impossibly worthwhile people.

The first time we played this game on the air ten or eleven years ago our list of would-be survivors included John Wayne, Billy Graham, Richard Nixon, Karl Menninger (of the mental clinic fame), and everyone's favorite guided-missile man, Werner von Braun. Almost everyone agreed that Nixon should go wading first, and this was, remember, years before he really fell into the water's gates. Dr. Menninger went second. Apparently, people figured a sound mind wouldn't be all that useful to a drowning body. Next came Billy Graham. Nothing personal, but everyone seemed to think that if anyone was ready to meet the big boss it was he. The Duke and

Werner were the last to go. A cowboy (no, actually only a pretend cowboy) and a guy who thinks up secret weapons? That really took some digesting.

The next day a few local Menningers put the unlikely choices in perspective for the rest of us. "Survival," they said, "is a human being's ultimate instinct. John Wayne and Werner von Braun were powerful symbolic father figures and protectors. It is perfectly natural for us to try to save those whom we expect in the final analysis to save us."

Wall, nyow, listen up pilgrim and listen up good. From now on I wantcha tuh rememba how big Wally and his faithful scouts in the sky got ya through the blizzards last winta, yuh-huh!

That survival thing evidently can also be used to explain throngs of gapers on the expressways, the crowds of curious who mill around the sites of major tragedies, the popularity of German Shepherds and Dobermans,* and other strange goings on. Seeing someone else's nightmare reassures us, because it shows that the potential tragedy didn't happen to us. At the risk of overstatement to the point of the absurd, the mind is an odd machine.

So, you are the only sailor on this boat, see? Your passengers include Jimmy Carter (where is Billy when we need him?), Pope John Paul II, Jonas Salk, Muhammad Ali, and your mom.

Who goes?

---

* The second and third most popular dogs in America. And why not? Can you imagine anything more lovable than your neighbor's Doberman? I once asked a lady whose Dobie had mauled and almost killed her how she had gotten rid of it, "Oh, I could never do that," she replied in horror.

Need some help with the life and death decision? Dr. Homer Johnson, chairman of the psychology department at Chicago's Loyola University, agreed to lend a hand last April. He had 123 of the department's students play the game. Fascinating isn't the word for their responses. Yes it is, absolutely fascinating.

Seventy-seven designated Muhammad Ali as the first to go swimming. Most specified his weight as the primary qualification for this dubious honor. Vote levels ranged from the low to the high teens for the Pope, the Pres, and the good doctor. Without fear of blowing the punch line, I'll give you 327 guesses as to why the majority of Jonas Salk's tossers chose him. "Because I have never even heard of this guy," was a typical explanation. Hardly anyone (two to be precise) could handle the idea of letting Mom go. The last two students abstained entirely; they said they would rather put it to a vote or sink together.

Now that you've had the benefit of all this input from the world of academe, let me rephrase the question. Who goes?

The Language
Lesson #4

Double Negatives Don't Hardly
Never Not Get the Job Done

As a boy, I lived in immediate proximity to the exception who proved this rule. Next door to him as well. His name was Orlando Jones, and his ability to convolute a perfectly straightforward statement was absolutely uncanny.

Orlando had spent the afternoon of our most memorable front porch conversation at his favorite uncle's house. I made the mistake of asking him if his uncle was a nice guy.

"You better not believe it," he replied. "That's the only place that I don't never go that I don't come back without not gettin' nothin'."

Last I heard of Orlando he was ghostwriting broadcast regulations for the FCC.

Radio Revisited

Many of the medium's observers think radio has one irreparable flaw—no pictures. Many of the medium's observers are mistaken. No pictures is no drawback. If anything, because the lack of a visual is also the lack of visual limitation, it is actually radio's biggest asset.

As near as modern chroniclers can estimate, intelligent communication dates back to the year 20236 B.C. One morning in early Grunk (May, for those of you who didn't major in Languages of the Paleolithic Era) of that year an enterprising young Neanderthal man stepped out of his cave after a long and particularly frustrating night and bellowed what was very probably the world's first promotional announcement. Students of the period have not yet been able to completely translate his message, but it evidently had something to do with the hairy lad's desire for a bit of companionship after a hard day at the tar pits. I have been allowed to personally monitor a tape of the event made by one of his neighbors down the canyon (the world's first stereo freak, no doubt). I was able to make out only a few garbled sounds. Please understand before going any further that the following transcript is the unofficial work of a totally untrained ear. The recording begins with a deep constant rumbling; breaks into what might, for lack of a more learned term, be called a series of heaving breaths; and finally explodes in an ear-shattering crescendo of what almost sounds like: "I WANT A WOMAN! I JUST GOTTA HAVE A WOMAN. UUUUGGGGHHHHHHHHHH!!!!" The depth and character of that "UUUUGGGGHHHHHHHH!!!!" revealed a little-known show biz tidbit. Jonathan Winters is probably a direct descendant of that caveman.

The man in the middle is named Jonathan Winters. He is a genius. The other two are named Roy Leonard and Wally Phillips. They are radio announcers. There is a big difference between geniuses and radio announcers.

We have come a long way from those humble beginnings. Today, multi-media presentations and satellite-relayed happenings bang at us from every direction. Through eons of progress, however, one basic fact has remained constant. Sound—simple, colorful, imagination-stretching sound, especially the sound of the human voice—has been, is, and will remain the single most effective form of communication known to man or woman or, better yet, both.

Radio, only radio, is sound, only sound. And it is free, so run right out and try some today!

Well, you didn't really expect to plow through this entire epic without being hit with at least one little commercial, did you? That would have been un-American.

Commerce, the art of buying and selling, has played an integral role in human activity ever since that same precocious guy in the fur coat traded his first filet of brontosaurus steak for someone else's two shiny rocks. It is the backbone of this country's economic system, such as it is.*

Yes, the radio which I perpetrate is commercial. I make no bones, pre-historic or otherwise, about it. No apologies either. If a product is good and its price is fair, what is wrong with saying so? Of course, the trick is making sure the product is good and the price is fair. It would be nice if I could say that I had not only used but was rabidly fond of every fantastic new something or other that I have ever done a spot for. It would also be a lie. Not even Victor Buono could eat, drink, and do that much in one lifetime.

There comes a point when you simply have to trust

---

* Except, perhaps, in Paducah, where it is illegal for merchants to physically drag customers off the street to make a sale.

someone. If a client whom you have learned to respect, or at least not suspect, is featuring some kind of revolutionary new pantyhose or erotic power tool or week-night disco emporium (none of which I have or had the slightest inclination to take advantage of), you either take it on faith or you get out of the business.

I hope that doesn't give you the impression that I'm willing to thump the tub for any promoter with a buck in his or her pocket. Ethics and common sense both preempt that notion. Radio stations can lose their licenses for indulging in false advertising, and on-air people can recommend drek to their listeners only so often before their credibility (that's a code word for livelihood) goes right down the chutes. In hopes of keeping their commercial acts clean, most radio stations have some very picky staff members whose sole function is to hang around stacks of rule books checking and rechecking products, services, and advertising claims made by advertisers. To the credit of a nice guy named Dan Pecaro, who is admittedly only in the broadcasting industry because he never quite mastered the art of putting major league curve balls into Comiskey Park's left field bleachers, the outfit I work for has such a hard-nosed continuity department that, for one reason or another, it actually turns away hundreds of thousands of dollars a year in potential commercial revenue. Dan Pecaro does not, by the way, happen to work in the station's sales department. He drives the boat.

Does that mean the place is perfect? Uh-uh. No matter how hard you work at it or how straight you try to play, a wild hare is still going to occasionally wiggle past the sentries.

I suppose there have been a few dogs that I never caught up with or, to be more precise, had catch up with me; but the one personal commercial Waterloogate I remember most vividly involved this (expletive deleted) "quaint, intimate" new restaurant on Chicago's "chic near-north side" which offered "subdued lighting, Mediterranean decor," and blah blah blah. On paper the place sounded like a slice of nirvana with cherries jubilee oozing down its sides. Fortunately or unfortunately, depending upon whether you happened to be the owner of the joint or someone with a distaste for ptomaine poisoning, a helpful listener knew the spot.

"You ever been there yourself?" he asked.

"Not yet, but I sure plan to try it soon," I replied.

"That is a real good idea, Wally. In fact, I would suggest you do that just as quickly as you can—certainly before it has another commercial scheduled." The man sounded like a man who knew something I didn't. That takes in almost everyone, and everyone is precisely who I wished I could have had along for lunch that day so I could have personally apologized.

I don't know exactly which part of the Mediterranean the interior decorators were trying to recapture, but I don't believe that I'll make it the destination of any of my next 312 dream vacations. The first thing I noticed was that its "chic near-north side" address was in immediate proximity to the chic near-north side addresses of several thriving porn bookshops, massage parlors, and their seamy like. Once inside and past the belch of a singularly unusual aroma, I encountered the source of its much-heralded "subdued lighting"—a couple of exposed bulbs hanging by their cords.* Shortly thereafter (I'm not sure how long it took me to sidestep the charming Dick But-

* Since Chicago law forbids eating in a place that is on fire, that subdued lighting has probably solved the problem by now.

THE WALLY PHILLIPS PEOPLE BOOK

kus look-alike maître d') one very embarrassed, more-than-slightly-ticked commercial deliverer (another code word for "unwitting huckster") beat a hasty retreat. He had an interesting chat with an eager radio account executive back at the ranch that afternoon.

Happily, such experiences have been very rare. For the most part, I've been on solid commercial ground. In the case of radio itself, which is what I think we were talking about a few thousand ill-chosen words ago, the glowing jabber and praise are definitely well-deserved. The thing is—the thing works.

Has any other pretended horror ever struck quite the same mass nerve or evoked anywhere near the same terrified response as Orson Welles's unintentionally realistic "War of the Worlds" broadcast in 1938? Thankfully not.

Will anyone who heard "Hawaii Calls" on 7 December 1941 ever forget the frozen crackle in announcer Webley Edward's voice as he pleaded with listeners not to think he was kidding around and shouted, "Goddamn it, this is for real!"

On an only slightly lighter note, can you fill in the blanks of the following famous advertisement:

"_____tastes good like a _____ should."

Most of you can. Do you realize how long it has been since you last heard those immortal words? Not since 1 January 1971. That is the date on which all cigarette advertising was banned from radio and television's public airwaves. Now those wonderful folks who bring you that most popular of all killer weeds haven't stopped advertising in the wake of the Surgeon General's "spurious accusations." They simply moved their hundreds of millions of dollars into alternative media of persuasion.

Can you remember Winston's current theme line? Neither can I. No loss.

Let's approach this from a different angle. I am thinking of a young adult female. She has blushing pink skin, an upturned nose, soft shoulders, plump, round thighs, trim ankles, a seductive grunt, and at the risk of indelicacy, a cute little tail. Her portrait is on the next page.

Radio lets the imagination run wild, encourages your mind to paint its own pictures. Sound, simple imagination-stretching sound, is all the canvas you'll ever need.

"Yeah, but to tell the whole story, you need something in black and white or four colors with a bleed to the edge of a double truck insert flyer special edition run," latter-day Neanderthals might say if they knew as little newspaper/print lingo as I do. "A customer can keep an ad around for days and reread it over and over. With radio, its here and gone in a minute. What can you say in a minute?"

How do the Preamble to the Constitution, the Lord's Prayer, the Pledge of Allegiance, and Julia Child's recipes for Emince du Beouf au Fromage y Crouton sound for openers?

How also does dropping the subject and leaving the business side of the business to those on its business side sound? Moved and seconded. Who says I never pay attention when Len O'Connor is talking about Chicago politics?

The Language
Lesson #5

Don't Say "'Deeze"
and "Dem"
and "Doze"

Unless, of course, you want to be a precinct committee-man in Chicago.

Now Let's Not

Radio can be such a personal communications medium that some people get the idea they can use it for personal communications. Not true. One of the several thousand official regulations which fill the FCC's eight-foot-thick regulations manual stipulates that the public airwaves may be used to communicate with anyone as long as they are not used to communicate with any one. To my amazement and your credit, we have generally managed to toe the swerving line rather well. I can only recall two blatant exceptions which seemed important enough at the times to warrant a wink at the rule book.

A lady, we'll call her Mary to muddy the waters, called one frosty autumn morning. A tremor in her voice indicated something more than small talk was on her mind.

"Wally, my husband is on his way to Springfield for a business meeting. I won't be able to reach him by phone until tonight, and that's going to be too late for him to avoid a very moving experience. I know he listens to you in the car. Can I give him an important message?"

I apologetically began to explain the rules and how radio stations are federally licensed and all, when I realized that I might be letting the abstract letter of a law mess up someone's life.

"Not really, Mary," I said, throwing caution to the management review committee, "but, if you could, what

Get Personal

would it be?" (Okay, score one for the committee.)

"Both my husband and our dog have been sick. Fred, my husband, has had the flu. Our dog is constipated. Both of their prescriptions came in small brown plastic bottles."

"I think I'm starting to get the message," I winced.

"I sure hope he does, because he doesn't have what he thinks he has in that suitcase. If he takes that medicine, it is going to be a very moving experience." At which point the poor concerned gal's tremor erupted into what almost sounded like convulsive laughter. Isn't it strange how your ears can play tricks on you?

Public service broadcasting in the truest sense of the word. Rivaled only by an even more urgent communiqué from a young mother of two on her unexpectedly early way back to the maternity ward.

"He's on the Dan Ryan right now, Wally. Please tell him that everything is fine. His mother is with the kids. I feel okay and I'll meet him at the hospital." It all happened so quickly, I didn't even get her name. Unfortunately, as a frantic caller a couple of minutes later made clear, neither did anyone else.

"Do you have any idea," he gulped, "how many guys there are on the Dan Ryan right now who have two kids and an expectant wife? I almost rammed a semi!"

Let me assure you, I have learned my lesson. That's it! No more worrying about what someone else is going to say that is against the rules for this kid. From now on, I'm not memorizing any more rules.

Of course, there isn't much I can do about the rules governing verbal taboos which I have already learned. Thanks primarily to one of George Carlin's irreverent past hippy-dippy weatherman-period routines, everyone has wanted a piece of this action recently. The FCC, NAB (National Association of Broadcasters), courts, and thousands of individual stations all agree that, society's changing mores notwithstanding, cussing on the radio is still a definite no-no. They particularly prohibit the on-air use of seven specific words. Ironically, hate, kill, steal, rape, lie, maim, and cheat are not among them. Yes, I know that rape is nothing but a dirty variation of one of the six proclaimed to be too dirty to utter. Don't look my way for logic. I just work here. That's not my job, man.*

I don't want to give the impression that we all live in mortal fear of accidentally stepping out of line. A typical broadcaster voices the equivalent of a short novel every time he or she does a stint. The law of averages is every bit as forceful as any other law. Do something often enough and you are eventually going to screw it up.† The mucks in charge know that and tend to look the other way when it happens. Some of them are even said to enjoy an occasional legitimate mistake. If you think those blooper record albums have some beauts, you ought to hear the reels most stations keep under lock and key.

* A prime candidate for Boot Hill that got away. Order it a stone. Might as well take care of "gross-out" and "heavy" while you're at it.

† If that isn't one of Murphy's laws, it ought to be.

You regulars know that I consider Lowell Thomas to be the breaking-up standard by which all others are judged. He didn't go often, but when he went, he went all the way. When something struck him as funny he would pause to savor the moment and then let out a quick, deep chuckle or two, another firmer chuckle, another pause, a false start, then heaving gasps, and finally, a rib-splitting groan. Totally infectious.

I've got too many favorites to begin to list them. Frankly, they don't translate all that well to paper anyway. You just have to hear the aforementioned Bob Bell sign-on a radio station at five in the morning by saying "the time at the tone will be ten o'clock" to appreciate it. And you had to know how genuinely uptight former Holy Cross/Notre Dame/Chicago Bear great George Connors was when he became one of broadcasting's first athlete color commentators and blurted, "Hello, George Connors, this is everyone."

It has happened to everyone in the business at one time or another, even to David Brinkley, as he proved to a national audience in early '79. Believe it or not, even Rick Rosenthal, the hard-driving young genius reporter who covers the world and other points of interest for us every morning, has had his ridiculously perfect voice melt into involuntary cackle once or twice. Just ask, "The Paptor of the Third Bastist . . . er, I mean . . . Paptist of the Third Bastor Church in St. Louis," whose sermonette he introduced one long-ago, he hoped-forgotten summer evening. Staff announcers and newsreaders are the most susceptible. Like designated pinch hitters or whatever Bill Veeck and his friends have decided to call them this season, they come into the action cold and are expected to get the juices flowing immediately. Ninety-nine times out of a hundred, professionalism and concentration pull it off. Given something like the following to rip 'n read, however, they have two chances—slim and none.

In addition to straight news stories, the various wire services, which almost all radio stations use to supplement their own news departments and many smaller ones rely upon *in toto*, often provide background material and human interest oddities to be used as stingers at the end of newscasts. This one is absolutely authentic. I defy you to read its first sentence without cracking a smile.

A002
  R A
    PM-FRY 4-21

ROCHESTER, N.Y. (UPI)—WAYNE MONAGAN WAS ARRESTED THURSDAY ON CHARGES OF ATTACKING A COP WITH A GREASY FRENCH FRY.

POLICE SAY OFFICER RAY MOSHER ENTERED AN ALL-NIGHT DINER AROUND 3 A.M. TO CALL HIS DISPATCHER. HIS OWN PORTABLE RADIO WAS BROKEN.

THE NEXT THING MOSHER KNEW, A KETCHUP-SOAKED FRENCH FRY BOUNCED OFF THE WALL NEAR HIM.

MOSHER EYED THE OFFENDER AND TOLD HIM TO STOP.

BUT A FRY FLEW AGAIN, THIS TIME AS MOSHER SAW THE MAN PULL BACK A FORK, "USING IT AS A CATAPULT" TO LAUNCH HIS MISSILE.

THE FRY HIT MOSHER ON THE LEFT SHOULDER, THE KETCHUP SPLATTERING HIS UNIFORM.

"THE SUBJECT WAS ARRESTED WHILE RELOADING," THE POLICE REPORT SAID.

MONAGAN, 26, WAS CHARGED WITH HARASSMENT
AND RESISTING ARREST AFTER MOSHER WRESTLED
HIM TO THE FLOOR AND SPRAYED HIM WITH MACE.

MONAGAN TOLD POLICE HE STARTED THE FRY
FIGHT BECAUSE MOSHER "GAVE HIM TICKETS IN
THE PAST."

UPI 04-21 12:16 AES

Now imagine yourself sitting in front of a live microphone with who knows how many listeners, including
the guy who owns the radio station.

You don't even need something inherently funny to do
you in. Juxtapose an innocent phrase, skip a line, read the
wrong lead-in to something you've been doing correctly
for years and, zap, you have the giggles. Your first reaction, naturally, is to try to suppress them. Fatal. The
more serious you try to sound, the funnier you know you
do. Pretty soon engineers, producers, and passers-by
whom they've invited off the street to watch the spectacle
are sadistically convulsing behind their secure, sound-
proof control room windows while you strangle on the
insistent tickle in your throat and try futilely to keep your
script from shaking. Regardless of the trigger's original
humor or lack of it, the experience can best be described
as one approximately as pleasant as the last appendec-
tomy you had without benefit of anesthesia.

At least the phenomenon is decent enough to be ecu-
menical. It strikes rock-jocks, wizened commentators,
sportscasters (especially sportscasters), talk show hosts,
staff announcers, and world-famous guest celebrities
without regard to race, creed, or programming format.
Even great orators and statesmen are not immune.

When Al Smith was the governor of New York, he

uttered the following beauty during a speech at Sing Sing Prison: "My fellow citizens," he began before realizing that convicts are not considered citizens, and corrected himself by saying, ". . . I mean, my fellow convicts." That wasn't right either, he realized, but with classic politico bravado he plowed ahead. "Well, anyhow, I'm glad to see so many of you here." Not exactly Johnny Cash material, but I'm sure it must have gotten a laugh from the boys in solitary.

Hubert Humphrey, no further introduction necessary, once exuberantly declared, "No sane person in this country likes the war in Vietnam, and neither does President Johnson!"

There was no way LBJ could take him to task for the slip of the tongue. He hog-tied himself when he drawled, "There are mothers and fathers all over this land. . . and I am one of those Mothers." It was said to be the last time he and Eugene McCarthy ever agreed on anything.

Remember the part a couple of pages ago where I said that I have too many favorite Bloopers to begin to list them? That was that part. This is this part. I've just decided that I have too many favorites *not* to begin to list them. Without further ado, whatever that is, the following are real-life lines spoken by real-life people under real-life excruciating circumstances:

"Stay tuned as Phillips's Magnesia presents 'Woman on the Run'"

"Remember, Friday is poultry night at the Gem Theater. All ladies will get a free goose. . . er, I mean, a free goose will be given to all the ladies."

"In the world of sports today, Yankee catcher Yogi Berra was hit on the head with a pitched ball. He was taken to the hospital for x-rays of his head. The x-rays showed nothing."

"We are not able to present our regularly scheduled program at this time so, due to a mistake, we bring you Liberace."

"See *Paleface* starring Bob Hope and lovely Jane Russell. Boy what a pair!"

"You will find your plane trip to Miami one of the greatest frights you've ever had."

"And here's a fashion note that will please the men. Women are not going to be wearing their clothes any longer this year."

"Tune in tomorrow when George finds he can no longer keep from Helen the serious condition of his business."

"This word from Washington comes from reliable White Horse souses."

"And now it gives me great pleasure to introduce you to the virgin of Governor's Island."

"This is NBC, the National Broadchasing Company."

"The vice-president, he said, would be the perfect man to lead a world-wide war on Hungary. I mean hunger."

"We are speaking to you live from the Municipal Auditorium. Tonight the season opens with a gala charity performance of Puccini's *La Bohème*. I see Mrs. Lucille Carter, the chairwoman of the Cultural

Committee, coming down the aisle. All eyes are upon her as she picks her seat."

"Hi-fiers, here's how you can improve your repro-duction."

My favorite cartoon says it all

The cartoon from *Pogo: We Have Met The Enemy And He Is Us* is Copyright © 1972 by Walt Kelly. Reprinted by permission of SIMON AND SCHUSTER, a Division of Gulf & Western Corporation.

They call it radio.

Once, it was almost strictly for entertainment.

Today it is, can be, and should be, an informer, companion, and an instrument of genuine one-to-one, people-to-people communication.

Tomorrow? I don't know. I know what I'd like it to be. I have a dream of a buzzing room full of producers, researchers, and about four hundred phones. Instant contact with the world. If something that people care about is happening over in Libya or out in Berwyn or anywhere else, I want to be there right now. I want to watch and help the miracle of people talking to each other quash the rumors, fill in the blanks, and let us get to know each other just the littlest bit better.

Impossible now.

But someday?

The Toughest Mystery of All Time

Mr. and Mrs. Jiggs finished breakfast as usual on Tuesday morning, and as usual, Mr. Jiggs planted a less-than-overheated marital kiss on Mrs. Jiggs's cheek before going to work. He got the family car out of the garage and started off. Halfway to the office, he stopped, turned the car around, and drove instantly home again. Upon arriving there, he drew a revolver and shot Mrs. Jiggs. How come?*

Answer: April fool, I'm not going to tell you! Oh, okay. There was a radio in Mr. Jiggs's car. As was his custom, he had it on as he drove. He was listening to a program that featured random calls to names listed in the local directory. Those who answered were asked to name their favorite radio station or some such tripe. To his surprise, he heard a call put through to his own telephone number. To his even greater surprise, the call was answered by a male voice—that of his best friend. The hot-tempered Mr. Jiggs jumped to conclusions.

This little game was for fun; that which follows is not.

* These "How Comes?" comes from a book appropriately titled *How Come?*

BANG! BANG! YOU'RE DEAD. Literally.

By our willingness to allow guns to be purchased at will and fired at whim, we have created an atmosphere in which violence and hatred have become national pastimes.

Dr. Martin Luther King, Jr.
November, 1963

With all the violence and murder and killings we've had in the United States, I think you will agree that we must keep firearms from people who have no business with guns.

Robert F. Kennedy
May 1968
five days before his assassination

This is going to make me a prime target, excuse the expression, of the National Rifle Association. That doesn't bother me a bit. The NRA bothers me a lot.

Wally Phillips
1979

THE WALLY PHILLIPS PEOPLE BOOK

Whether it has succeeded or not, most of this book has tried to be light, perhaps even entertaining. Not here, not now. There is nothing light or entertaining about the insanity of the handgun situation in this country. For the record, please note that I said handgun. I have no argument with sportsmen, hunters, collectors, or other legitimate long-barrel enthusiasts. My concern is over the weapon that has only one function—killing people.

I could no more write the rest of this chapter unemotionally than those of you who already have an opinion diametrically opposite mine could read it that way. I won't even try. For the remainder of you, here are some facts to chew on. Make your own decision.

There are more than 50 million handguns in circulation in the United States. The vast majority of them are inexpensive, deadly Saturday Night Specials. There is one sold every thirteen seconds. They are involved in more than fifty percent of all the murders committed in this country.

There are more people killed by gunfire in this country annually than in the rest of the free world combined. Think there's any connection?

Consulate estimates of handgun ownership per 100,000 population are as follows:

Ireland	under 500
Finland	under 500
Netherlands	under 500
Greece	under 500
Great Britain	under 500
Yugoslavia	500-1,000
Israel	1,000
Austria	3,000
Canada	3,000
America	13,500

BANG! BANG! YOU'RE DEAD. LITERALLY.

There are more people killed by gunfire in this country in an average day than in England, Wales, and Japan in a year.

There are more than four times as many people killed by gunfire annually in Houston, Texas than in England, Wales, and Japan combined.

There are more than twenty times as many people killed by gunfire in Boston, a city of less than a million, than in London, a city of more than eight million.

We probably ought to take it with a grain of salt, but neither Russia nor China report any gun homicides at all.

Over 200,000 people are injured, robbed, or raped at the business end of a handgun every year.

There are 10,000 handgun suicides and 3,000 accidental handgun deaths in this country every year.

During the peak years of the Vietnam war, 42,300 Americans died in combat. During the same period, more than twice as many were murdered with handguns in the United States.

More Americans have been shot to death with handguns on our own streets than have died in all the wars this country has ever fought.

More than forty percent of those who die from gunfire are nineteen or under.

A few years ago, a phantom killer called Legionnaires Disease took a couple of dozen lives. The federal government rightly launched an all-out campaign to identify and eradicate the mystery virus. Guns take 25,000 American lives a year, every year. We do nothing.

Why?

The Constitution? Apparently not. The Supreme Court has ruled four separate times that it does not guarantee the right to personal gun ownership.

Protection from home invaders and other criminals?

Well, three out of four gun-related killings are committed by friends and acquaintances during moments of unpremeditated rage. An average of ten innocent people die for every intruder apprehended or shot with a privately owned handgun. Six of the ten are family members of the gun's owner—most of them children.

Public opinion? Hardly. Every poll of the general public that I have seen indicates that a vast majority of Americans want stricter gun control legislation enacted. A Harris Poll in 1975 put the vote at seventy-seven percent.

The NRA? Could be. It is organized, vocal, well-financed and politically active. It is supposedly the fourth most effective lobbying group in the country and invested 1.3 million dollars in 1978 election campaigns of pro-gun senators and congressmen. I can certainly attest to its ability to tie up a radio show's phone lines. Get them started and you might as well close up shop.

Those are some, just some, of the nauseating facts. To my mind they are all too simple, all too clear. What matters is what you, not I, think. I have already said my piece. If you want something done about this cancer in our society, let the people you keep in office know. If you aren't sure and want to hear more before making your decision, write to one of the following absolutely biased, absolutely correct organizations:

The National Gun Control Center
P.O. Box 32335
Washington D.C. 20007

National Coalition to Ban Handguns
100 Maryland Ave. N.E.
Washington D.C. 20002

BANG! BANG! YOU'RE DEAD. LITERALLY.

The Committee for the Study of Handgun Misuse
109 N. Dearborn Street
12th floor
Chicago, Illinois 60602

Sorry to have turned so heavy on you. I am obviously not in a business in which alienating powerful special interest groups or anyone else makes much sense. I know that these pages have done precisely that to some of you. I had to do it. You see, I have a daughter and a son and a daughter. Whether you like it or not, I want them to be able to grow up in a country and a world where they can walk down a street, any street, without having to worry about getting their heads blown off. I had to do this for Holly and Todd and Jennifer. What are the names of the people you love?

Loose Ends

If I ever write another book, I shall tell all about a few other fabulous characters you have known, including Ernie Banks, Bill and Mary Frances Veeck, Gary Deeb, the private citizens Bilandic, Aaron Gold, Merrill Chase, Bene Stein, Rhonda Fleming, Mickey Rooney, Bill Kurtis, Forrest Tucker, the late unexaggeratedly great Lou Zahn, Bob Conrad, Burt Reynolds, Rich Little, Herman Franks, Bill Berg, Don Kessinger, Judge Abe Marovitz, George Halas, Arnold Morton, Bill Contos, Gene Sage, Eli Shulman, Don Roth, Rich Melman, Vic Gianotti, Jovan Trboyevic, Jean Banchet, Harry Melnick, Don DeCarlo, Barbara Eden, Chuck Fegert, Bob Greene, Jack McHugh, Red Passerella, Jim Finks, Pat Boone, Johnny Mathis, Dionne Warwick, Johnny & Jeannie Morris, Joan Rivers, Red Grange, Kate Smith, Alyce Salerno, Ara Parseghian, Bobbe & Lou Goldblatt, Digger Phelps, Ed Moran, Jay and Ed McGreavy, Sam Karoll, Bart Starr, Paul Hornung, Brent Musberger, Orion Samuelson, Dom DiFrisco, Val Kilkeary, Sandi Freeman, Maggie Daly, Ray Sons, Roger Ebert, Gene Siskel, Alan Schwartz, Dan

Musser, Ed Hennessy, Victor Lownes, Gene Sullivan, Jerry Hearn, Marilyn Lelani Smith, Bill Hickey, Bill Friedkin, Miriam Edwards, Frank Parker, Lucille Ball, Christie Hefner, Mort Rosen, Steve Foley, Dick Darke, Jerry Casper, John Cotter, Dan Nikolich, Mary Mills, Stormy Bidwell, Seymour Paisin, Frank Cizon, Don O'Brien, Dan Devine, Harry the Horse, Henry Gardner, Irv Seaman, Bernie Polek, Virginia Russett, Austin Butner, Nick Dispensa, Stan Mikita, Vince Lloyd, Bob Sirott, Bob Collins, Milt Rosenberg, Jerry Kovler, and (Ibnl) Lou Boudreau.

This page probably seems to have been added for no particular reason. Not so. It has been added to make your futile search for the five-grand name in the little black box that much more impossible. Little did you know I was such a nasty so

So Who Ever Said We Were Perfect?

"Bam! Bam! Bam! Bam! Four shots ripped through my gut and I was off on the greatest adventure of my life."

No, I'm not going to put you through an instant replay of the last gory chapter. This is the way a funny book by a funny guy named Max Shulman began. It still does begin that way as a matter of fact. Ask someone who doesn't know any better to peg the story's locale and, more likely than not, you will hear "Chicago." No thanks, I imagine, to the unending popularity of *Untouchables* reruns, our largely undeserved reputation has spread far and wide. It once happened to a friend of mine all the way over in Greece.

Two of his dining companions on an island cruise spoke only French. "Paris?" my friend gestured in hopes of establishing some base of common reference.

"No, no, Nice," the lady responded while her husband or whatever (you know how those French are) chuckled. The idea of being presumed a Parisian had apparently struck him as funny. Stereotyping must be international.

"I . . . am . . . from . . . Chicago," my friend said very

slowly. As you no doubt already know, speaking a foreign language very slowly makes it easier to understand. It's the same principle as shouting to a blind person with perfect hearing who is two feet away.

"Ooh." Her eyes lit with recognition as she held up both hands in reasonable facsimile of a machine gun and said, "Boom, Boom, Boom."

Wrong. Let me rephrase that. WRONG!

Hey, Chicago is a big city. It has the same problems of pollution, crime, congestion, and pot holes that any other big city on this or any other planet has. No more. Perhaps less.

Sure, Al Capone stunk up the joint forty years ago. (He actually hung out more in Cicero and Cal City, but they're close enough for out-of-towners.) Yes, Richard Speck and John Gacy did earn their infamy here. Yes, the thought of it is enough to turn your stomach. No, the reality of their contributions to our scene cannot and should not be dismissed, but they shouldn't be allowed to forever defame and defile it either.

With absolutely no intention of minimizing our very real problems, I simply wish people from Nice and Schenectady and everywhere else would occasionally get a glimpse of what this place is really all about. Chicago, and I'm obviously including Park Ridge and Whiting and Oak Brook and all the rest of its unofficial parts (like Illinois, Wisconsin, Indiana, Michigan, Iowa, etc.) in the bargain whether they like it or not, is simply a livable corner of the world.

It is also an architectural wonderland, a meteorologist's dream, and the only place on earth that can and usually does turn out five million paying fans a year to rabidly cheer for professional athletic teams that haven't won any laurels in more than one hundred combined years of competition.

The official Chamber of Commerce stats are every bit as impressive as you would expect them to be. They show Chicago to be the world's number one air travel center, candy manufacturer, convention headquarters, domestic exports leader, furniture seller, meat processor, and maker of steel, appliances, musical instruments, radios and televisions, canned and frozen foods, lamp shades, diesel engines, fabricated wire, screws and bolts, telephone equipment, and so on for about ten or eleven more pages. Chicago is the site of the world's tallest apartment building, biggest office building, and everythingest any other kind of building. It has the world's busiest street corner and several of the most congested expressways.

But more important by far, Chicago is a people place. A warm, caring, human place. For every Capone, Gacy, or Speck it is home to hundreds of thousands of O'Goreks, Morales, Suzukis, Kaszas, Carrs, Kuffels, Howards, Brnes, Frugolis, Mahoneys, Baabs, Nudelmans, Glochowskys, Astrins, Getzs, and Washingtons. They aren't famous, rich, or politically connected. They're just people. People who push each other's cars out of snowdrifts, bet on the World Series, raise kids, pay the bills, and care about each other. They're people who are willing to lend a hand when it's needed.

Chicago is people like Rita Malloy. (I hope I have the right name on this one. My file folders tend to intermarry after a while.) Rita or Bridget, I'm sure it was one or the other, was sitting aboard an airplane at Ireland's Shannon Airport one day and overheard a fellow passenger, a young mother with twin babies in her arms, pleading and frantically explaining to a steward that she didn't realize the regulations prohibited her from holding more than one infant in her lap while the machine was in flight.

She, the young mother that is, called me the next morning to tell the story and publicly thank her new friend who had volunteered to fly all the way across the ocean with a complete stranger's baby bouncing, wiggling, and probably wetting in her lap.

Chicago is people named Marcia and Matt and Claudia and hundreds whose names end with "ski" who made it possible for a confused, frightened man to embrace his family.

Antoni Piakowski, a laborer, had saved his wages for years so that he might bring his wife and child here from Poland. A smooth-talking travel agent had heard about his plans, taken his money (more than $4,000), and promised to make all the necessary arrangements. You can smell it coming, can't you? The bum skipped town.

I spoke to Antoni's landlady one morning (he didn't speak or understand much English) and only half-kiddingly suggested that we should impose a surtax of about two cents a head on the members of Chicago's immense Polish-American community to help make his dream come true. Two weeks later, Antoni had $5,300 in his pocket, a family on the way, and a special feeling for a special new home in his heart.

Another all-too-similar incident arose just last May. The eighth graders of St. George's School in Tinley Park, one of Chicago's great southwest suburban neighborhoods, had planned, worked, and saved all year for a graduation trip to Florida. Less than a week before their eagerly-awaited departure date, the teacher who had volunteered to coordinate this logistical nightmare of an adventure learned that some lowlife had done a disappearing act with virtually the entire $16,000 travel fund. She was understandably frantic. With three nuns, a priest, and their charge of impressionable young minds on the verge of one of the greatest disappointments of their lives, she didn't know where to turn for help.

Then she thought of you.

The story's happy ending is as predictable as it is heartwarming and spectacular. You came through again. You donated dozens of items to be auctioned on the air in the children's behalf; then you bought them back at better than market value. You taught some future leaders and the rest of us a lesson in a way that no textbook ever could. You showed them that people care.

Stories of your incredible willingness to help each other out of big jams and small jams would quite literally fill another book. The most obvious of them, and the one I simply cannot ignore here, is your response to the Neediest Kids Christmas Fund.

This magnificent adventure grew out of the realization by Family Services caseworkers a few years ago that the subsistence checks they delivered were in many cases precisely what the term implies. They covered the bare minimum of their recipients' physical necessities—period. There was simply no way a deserted woman's budget would allow the luxury of a Christmas for her children. The workers started taking up a collection out of their own pockets to buy candy canes, oranges, and socks. Festive stuff, huh? It wasn't long before the city's unofficial vice-president in charge of caring, Norman Ross, heard of their efforts, spread the word, and created a mechanism with his bank and others for turning the spirit into a fact. The rest is history. The rest is also too good to be true. Do you have any idea how many candy canes, not to mention sweaters and shoes and even dolls and baseballs, a million dollars a year can buy? Not enough, but one hell of a lot more than those kids ever would have seen without you.

We're not talking about antiseptic grants from computerized charitable foundations. They are wonderful in their own right, but nowhere near as special as the real people like you who have sent in quarters and dollars and fives and tens and office party pools and cuss box collections and greeting card budgets year after year. There have been thousands of you. Hundreds of thousands. A few, like those who attached these letters to their love, have said it all.

$10.00

Dear Mr. Phillips:

Pleasd gi ve this mon ey to dso o m e n eedy ki s
from my Winnie Th e Poo hh B ank

BOBRUTI, JR.

P.S. I'm 4 years old & I c an typ e .

237

DEAR WALLY ———

NOVEMBER 25TH MY MOM DIED. BEING
OF THE JEWISH FAITH, WE HAVE A MOURNING
PERIOD CALLED SHIVAH.

FOR THREE DAYS FRIENDS OF
OURS COOKED FOR OUR FAMILY, SERVED
US & GUESTS, AND ALSO CLEANED. IT
IS TO HONOR THEM THAT I AM ENCLOSING
A CHECK FOR YOUR NEEDIEST KIDS. THEY
ALL LISTEN TO YOUR SHOW & I SURE
WOULD APPRECIATE IT IF YOU WOULD
MENTION THEIR NAMES ON YOUR SHOW
SOMETIME DURING THE WEEK BETWEEN
7:15 & 8:00 A.M. THANK YOU ——

Jerry Lipschultz

NORMA WEINBERG
NORMA COHEN & DAUGHTER BARBARA
RUTH MARKS
BESS WOLFSON $50
MILLIE MAURER
FAY DRUCIC
EDNA COHEN
FLORENCE KREITZLER
ROZZELLA COOPER.

Fraternal Order of Police

CHICAGO LODGE NO. 7

December 8, 1977

Mr. Wally Phillips
% Miss Marilyn Miller
WGN
2501 Bradley Place
Chicago, Illinois

Dear Mr. Phillips:

Much of the public views Police Officers as "Hard and Callus Individuals", but one thing that can break through this hard and callus impression is a child, especially a child in need.

On behalf of the Fraternal Order of Police I take great pleasure in enclosing a check for $370 to your Neediest Children Fund. $300 is donated from the funds of the Fraternal Order of Police, Chicago Lodge No. 7 and the additional $70 is a collection which was taken up at our meeting on December 5th.

$370

Wishing you and all your Neediest Children a very happy holiday season from the members of the Fraternal Order of Police, Chicago Lodge No. 7, I remain,

Fraternally.

FRATERNAL ORDER OF POLICE
CHICAGO LODGE NO. 7

John Dineen
President

**mayfair
pantry
pretties**

December 8, 1977

Dear Wally,

The Mayfair Pantry Pretties are proud and happy to present you with a
che$k for $1,500.00 (!!) for the Neediest Children's Fund.

Thanks to your phone call, several people came to Ferrara Manor the
night of our Put-Ons Fashion Show who would have otherwise never heard
about us.

Besides raising these funds, the 500 in the audience (plus the waitresses,
bar tenders, washroom attendants, busboys and the hired help from the
party going on upstairs) seemed to have a dynamite evening. The response
was incredible. I would even go so far as to say if the audience enjoyed
it half as much as we did, then _we_ enjoyed it twice as much as they did!

So you see Wally, your campaign for funds for the Neediest Children was
a three-way benefit. The performers had a ball, the audience was wined,
dined, and royally entertained, and the Neediest Children will have a
Merrier Christmas.

We thank you for giving us the opportunity to be a part of a most joyful
enterprise.

Ornamentally yours, Diane

The Pretties 4850 46 N. Kildare (Diane Scholler)

Dear Wally,

Once again I appreciate the chance to send a small but loving contribution to your fund.

Wally you can't know how great it is to hear so many kind and caring messages your friends send with their contributions. My little girl and I are Public Aid Recipients and we've both taken verbal abuse from time to time because of it. Sometimes I stand at the cashier check out at a Super-Market so embarrassed when people have to wait a little longer because of my food stamps that I want to just fall in a hole in the floor if only there was one there. Or, to present your Green Medical card for a doctors receptionist or pharmacist and have people take a careful look at you and try to figure out what your problem is, and sometimes even ask! Your fund and all the calls and mail you get makes me realize that there ARE hundreds of people who really do understand and not only keep an open mind, but an open heart too. Thank you Wally for helping towards a better understanding for us. We don't like our circumstances and pray it will not last. For a person who worked all their lives to be in this position is very hard. But, you have shown that there are people out there with the true spirit of what Christmas is all about and they care.

God love you Wally Philips,
Sincerely, Connie Hynes

No, I don't think our friends from Nice understand at all. Bad news and aberrations like Capone, Speck, Gacy, and the handful of lunatics who wanted to march on Skokie aren't what this country or this city is all about. You are. I sure hope you're as proud and happy to have known you as I am.

Appendix
The List of Books

A treasury of painstakingly-collected literary disarmament guaranteed to make you the hit of the car pool, a must invite on low society's cocktail party circuit, and if worse comes to worse, the survivor of your very own radio show.

On the subject of pure, unadulterated **Trivia** in absolutely no logical order, which is as it should be:

Fascinating Facts: David Louis; Ridge Press/Crown, 1977.

Have You Ever Wondered?: Jerome Beatty, Jr.; Macfadden, 1962.

Whatever Became Of (volumes I through IV): Richard Lamporski; Ace/Crown/Bantam.

What Happened To: Patrick Agan; Ace, 1974.

The Guinness Book of World Records: Norris and Ross McWhirter.

Dunlop's Illustrated Encyclopedia of Facts: the McWhirters; Bantam.

The Book of Lists: David Wallechinsky and Irving and Amy Wallace; Bantam, 1978.

Famous First Facts and Records: Joseph Nathan Kane; Ace, 1975.

Best, Worst, and Most Unusual: Bruce Fenton and Mark Fowley; Fawcett, 1975.

Trivia: A Compendium of Useless Information: Timothy Fullerton; Hart, 1976.

Sneaky Feats: Tom Farrell and Lee Eisenberg; Pocket Books.

Glad You Asked That: Marilyn and Hy Gardner; Ace.

Durations: The Encyclopedia of How Long Things Take: Stuart Sandow; Times Books.

More Best, Worst, and Most Unusual: same guys.

The Book of Strange Facts and Useless Information: Scott Monis; Doubleday.

Trivia: Edwin Goodgold and Dan Carlinsky; Dell, 1966.

Radio

The Big Broadcast: Frank Buxton and Bill Owen; Avon, 1977.

Who Was That Masked Man?: David Rothel; Barnes.

But That's Not What I Called to Ask: Hilly Rose.

Paul Harvey's The Rest of the Story: Paul Aurandt; Doubleday.

The Tube

So You Think You Know TV: Donald Kennedy; Ace, 1971.

The Star Trek Quiz Book: Bart Andrews and Brad Dunning; Signet, 1977.

The World's Greatest TV Quiz: Tom Bornhauser and Dennis Palumbo; Berkley, 1974.

The TV Guide TV Quiz Book: Stan and Fred Goldstein; Bantam, 1978.

The Quiz Show Quiz Book: Frank W. Chimnock; Berkley, 1977.

The Official TV Trivia Quiz Book: Bart Andrews; Signet, 1975.

TV Movies: Leonard Martin; Signet, 1979.

The Television Years: Arthur Shulman and Roger Youman; Popular Library, 1973.

The Other Reason Drive-Ins Are Popular

The American Movies Reference Book: Paul Michael; Prentice Hall, 1970.

Academy Awards Illustrated: Robert Osborne; ESE, 1974.

Hollywood's Great Love Teams: James Robert Parrish; Arlington House, 1974.

The Compleat Motion Picture Quiz Book and

Son of the Compleat Motion Picture Quiz Book: Harry and Yolanda Trigg; Doubleday, 1975 and 1977.

A New Pictorial History of the Talkies: Daniel Blum; Putman.

The Real Stars: Leonard Martin; Curtis.

So You Think You Know Movies: Donald Kennedy; Ace, 1970.

The Oscar Quiz Book: Stanley Hopman; Dale/Caroline, 1978.

The Filmgoer's Companion: Leslie Halliwell; Hill & Wang.

The Filmgoer's Book of Quotes: Arlington House.
The Great Movie Stars: The Great Years: Leslie, again; David Shipman; Crown.
The Movies: Richard Griffith and Arthur Mayer; Bonanza.

The Greatest Place in the World Ever Named After the Smell of Onions

Is There Only One Chicago?: Kenan Heise; Westover, 1973.
Illinois Architecture: Frederick Koeper; University of Chicago Press, 1968.
Sweet Home Chicago: Tem Horwitz; Chicago Review Press, 1977.
Clout: Len O'Connor; Henry Regnery Company, 1975.
Boss: Mike Royko; New American Library, 1971.
The New Good But Cheap Chicago Restaurant Book: Jill and Ron Rohde; Swallow Press, 1977.
Chicago's How To Do It Guide: the Back of the Yards Council.
The Chicago Guide Book: Chicago Magazine; Regnery, 1972.
Chicago: Creating New Traditions: Chicago Historical Society.
Chicago: Nicolai Canetti; Haddington House.
Norman Mark's Chicago: Norman Mark; Chicago Review Press.
Dining in Chicago: Karen Goldwich Stevens; Peanut Butter Press.
Chicago Gourmet: Sue Kupcinet and Connie Fish; Simon & Schuster, 1977.

Chicago: A Pictorial History: Herman Kogan and Lloyd Wendt; Bonanza Books.
How To Survive in Chicago and Enjoy It: Barre Westover.
Chicago: The Growth of a Metropolis: Harold Mayer and Richard Wade; Universiy of Chicago Press.

Things That Bounce, Soar, Spiral, Dribble and Dominate Our Lives

Guinness Sports Record Book: Norris and Ross McWhirter; Bantam.
The Sports Nostalgia Quiz Book: Zander Hollander and David Schultz; Signet.
Great Black Athletes: The Reynolds Company.
Cooper Rollow's Bears '78: Cooper Rollow; Caroline House, 1978.
The Runners Guide to Chicago: Tem Horwitz; Chicago Review Press.

More of the Same with the Emphasis on Humiliation

Watch the Ball, Bend Your Knees, That'll Be $20 Please: Ed Collins; Caroline House, 1977.
Golfer's Stroke Saving Handbook: Craig Shanklad; Signet.
Who's Who in Golf: Len Elliot and Barbara Kelly; Haddington House.
Golf Is Madness: Ted Barnett; Simon & Schuster.

It's Only Funny If They Laugh

The Essential Lenny Bruce: John Cohen; Ballantine.
Comic Epitaphs from the Very Best Old Grave-
    yards: Peter Pauper Press.
Humor in the Headlines: Earl Temple; Pocket Books,
    1969.
Classified Humor: Earl Temple; Pocket Books, 1970.
Crossovers: Russ Fisher; Laughter Library, 1977.
How To Break 90 Before You Reach It: Steve Brody;
    North River Press.
A Loser Is . . . : Charlie Manna and Bill Majeski; Simon,
    1968.

A Name by any Other Name Is Still a Name

American Surnames: Eleson C. Smith; Chilton, 1969.
The Name Game: Christopher P. Andersen; Simon &
    Schuster, 1977.
First Names First: Leslie Alan Dunkling; Universe.
Name Your Baby: Lareina Rule; Bantam, 1963.
What Not to Name the Baby: Roger Price and Leonard
    Stern; Price, Stern, Sloan, 1960.
Never Name Your Baby Bill: Price, Stern, Sloan.

Music and Other Interesting Noise

The Rolling Stone Illustrated History of Rock 'n
    Roll: Rolling Stone.
The Official Rock 'n Roll Trivia Quiz Book: Marc Sad-
    kin; Signet.
My Country 'tis O Thee: Harper & Row.

The Pushbutton Telephone Songbook: Michael Scheff; Price, Stern, Sloan.
Music of the Whole Earth: David Reck; Scribner's.
An Almanac of Words at Play: Willard R. Espy; Potter.
Strictly Speaking: Edwin Newman; Simon & Schuster.
Such Language!: Otto Whittaker; Drake House, 1967.
The Official CB Language Dictionary: Lanie Dills; Dills, 1977.
Horsefeathers: Charles Earle Funk; Warner Paperback, 1972.

Inside the Little Lines

Light from Many Lamps: Lillian Eichler Watson; Pocket, 1976.
Guidewords: Miriam C. Hunter; Shaw Barton.
The 1811 Dictionary of the Vulgar Tongue: Digest Books.
Confucius Say
The New Book of Unusual Quotations: Rudolph Flesch; Harper Row.
The Holy Bible

And a Little of Everything Else

Time: July 4, 1776: Commemorative issue.
The Family Album: Arthur and Nancy DeMoss; Family Album.
Parents' Magazine Christmas Holiday Book: Yorke Henderson, Lenore Miller, Eileen Gaden, Arnold Freed; *Parents'* Magazine.

The American Heritage Dictionary of the English Language
The World Book Dictionary
The Oxford Educational Dictionary
The Twentieth Anniversary Playboy Reader: Hefner; Playboy.
Snapping (America's Epidemic of Personality Change): Flo Conway and Jim Siegelman; Lippincott.
The Book of Numbers: Heron House.
Male Sexuality: Bernie Zilbergard, Ph.D.; Little, Brown.
Just Because They're Jewish: M. Hirsh Goldberg; Stein & Day.
Mindstyles/Lifestyles: Nathaniel Lande; Price, Stern, Sloan.
The Shark Book: Sandra D. Romashko; Windward, 1974.
The People's Almanac: David Wallechinsky and Irving and Amy Wallace; Doubleday.
Birds of North America: Chandler Robbins; Golden Press.
A Billion Dollars: James T. deKay; Evans, 1977.
The Farmer's Almanac: Almanac Publishing.
Can Elephants Swim?: Robert M. Jones; Time-Life, 1969.
CB Lingo: Kevin Cronin; CB Specialities.
The Dictionary of Misinformation: Tom Burnam; Ballantine, 1975.
Murphy's Law
The Official Rules
The World Almanac: Doubleday.
Astrological Almanac: Lynne Palmer; Jove, 1977.

The Book of Chinese Chance: Suzanne White; Fawcett Crest.

The Nice Thing About Living Alone

Good News/Bad News Book: Martin A. Rodeway; Price, Stern, Sloan.

Xaviera's Supersex: Xaviera Hollander; Signet.

The Cold Weather Catalog; Doubleday Dolphin.

Laughlin's Fact Finder: William Laughlin; Parker.

Happy Birthday: Ed Simpkins; Box 220, Prior Lake, Minn.

2,000 Insults for All Occasions

2,000 More Insults for All Occasions: Louis Safian; Pocket.

Games for the Super Intelligent

How Come?

The Black Culture Quiz: Roscoe Brown Ph.D.; Sperry Hutchins.

Women in America: Geraldine Whitelhead; Sperry Hutchins.

The Terror Chronicle: Bob and Sandy Sang; Sang Pub.

Winning at the Casino Table: Terrence Reese; Signet.

Jewish Low Calorie & Cholesterol Cookbook: Robert Leviton; Signet.

The Encyclopedia Britannica Quiz Book: Pocket Books; 1973.

The All-Star Turnabout Quiz Book: Mark Tan; Price, Stern, Sloan.

The Encyclopedia of American Facts and Dates: Thomas Crowell.

Bloodletters and Badmen: Jay Robert Nash; M. Evans, 1973.

Are You Superstitious?: Lore Gowan; Pocket Books, 1970.

The Compleat Art of Public Speaking: Jacob Braude; Bantam, 1970.
American Cookery: James Beard; Little Brown.
The Ascent of Man: J. Bronowski; Little Brown.
The Encyclopedia of Wines: Alexis Lichine.
Gambler's Digest: Clement McQuade; Digest Books.
Riverview: Chuck Wlodarczyk; Schori Press.
Nostalgia Catalogue: Jim Harmon; Tarcher/Hawthorn.
How To Do Almost Everything Else: Bert Bacharach; Simon & Schuster.
The Supernatural: Douglas Hill and Pat Williams; Plume.
Thank You for the Giant Sea Tortoise: Mary Ann Madden; Viking.
An Eccentric Guide to the United States: James Dale Davidson; Berkley/Westover.
Barbarians in Our Midst: Virgil W. Peterson; Atlantic.
Dillinger: Dead or Alive: Jay Robert Nash and Ron Offen; Regnery.
Sinatra: Arnold Shaw; Holt, Rinehart, Winston.
The Show Business Nobody Knows: Earl Wilson; Cowles.
The Facts of Wife: Robert Warren; Rodney.
Secrets of Magic: Walter B. Gibson; Grosset & Dunlop.
The Dog Catalog: R.V. Denenberg and Eric Seidman; Today Press.
Fascinating Stories from Yesterday: John Hurst and Judith Tom; Mid-America.
The Trenton Pickle Ordinance: Dick Hyman: Stephen Greene Press.